It Won't Be Easy

It Won't Be Easy

AN EXCEEDINGLY HONEST (AND SLIGHTLY UNPROFESSIONAL) LOVE LETTER TO TEACHING

Tom Rademacher

FOREWORD BY *Dave Eggers*

University of Minnesota Press | Minneapolis | London

Published by the University of Minnesota Press
111 Third Avenue South, Suite 290
Minneapolis, MN 55401-2520
http://www.upress.umn.edu

ISBN 978-1-5179-0112-7 (pb)
A Cataloging-in-Publication record for this book is available from the Library of Congress.

Printed in the United States of America on acid-free paper

The University of Minnesota is an equal-opportunity educator and employer.

22 21 20 19 18 17   10 9 8 7 6 5 4 3 2 1

TO MY FAMILY,
TO THE FAMILY,
AND TO ALL MY RIDE OR DIE

Contents

Foreword

Dave Eggers

He is fourteen years old. He is covered in zits. There are zits so big on his face that they obscure his vision. This can happen. There can be a growth on a young man's nose that actually impedes his vision, like a thumb blocking a camera lens.

This young man with the vision-obscuring zits is somehow not so popular with the young women in his school. He is not happy about this, and he is not happy about being hopelessly late to puberty, and not happy about being cut from the tennis team, and that his home is loud and his parents fight and his dad drinks too much, and that the many times he's run away have gotten him nowhere.

He is angry about all this, and he is angry about his foot odor. His foot odor is so bad that people know he is coming far before they see him. They actually smell him and his shoes coming. His mother insists he keep his shoes outside, in the garage, even during a Chicago winter, so when he puts them on, they are frozen but no less foul. His foot-odor problem is so bad that one of his best friends at the time is another young man with terrible foot odor. They met, in the locker room after gym class, because they were both trying to put foot-odor powder in their shoes and bonded over what worked and what didn't.

This young man is angry, confused, and spends far too much time listening to Morrissey and riding his bike late at night. He hangs out with other rebellious young men, and together they commit uncountable acts of petty vandalism. They don't do terrible things, but they do stupid things that could, in a few years, become dangerous acts.

He is a sophomore in high school, and in the fall he has to take a yearlong English class. The second semester of the class involves studying the contemporary novel, but the first semester is called Public Speaking. It's the sophomore English requirement, and this young man has no interest at all in this class, which will require him to stand before his peers, with his enormous zits, to stand up and be looked at, when he wants only to be away, to be invisible.

But the teacher is funny. The teenager is a fan of Monty Python, and this teacher, with his dry wit, seems like he would like Python, too. On the first day of class, there is another student, a red-haired young man named Hank, who announces to the teacher that from now on he'd like to be called "Hans." The teacher accepts this readily. "You're going Old World on us, huh?" the teacher says, and after that calls Hank "Hans." This small allowance registers with the zit-covered young man. Interesting, he thinks.

The first assignment in the class is to write a persuasive speech. The students in the class are asked to come up with a proposal for their persuasive speech and present it to the teacher, who will make sure it's worthy of pursuing.

Other students propose speeches about standard persuasive things, like legalizing marijuana or a law forbidding the burning of the American flag. The teenage boy, though, feeling rebellious, decides he will challenge the teacher. So for his persuasive speech he proposes that he will try to convince the class that they should take a bicycle trip to the inner mantle of the earth. The teenager has thought of only one real reason that taking a bicycle trip to the inner mantle of the earth would be a good idea, and that reason is that a trip like that would be downhill, all the way.

So the teenager thinks he's pretty clever. And he expects the teacher to fight him on this. After all, the teenager is used to fighting at home. He fights every day with his father, so why shouldn't he fight with his teacher?

The teenager challenges the teacher with his ludicrous proposal, and instead of resistance, the teacher, in his dry-witted way, nods and says, "Well, that makes a certain sense. You've convinced me already."

And he allows the teenager to write his persuasive speech about the appeal of biking to the inner mantle of the earth.

Now. I want to stop here and explain what just happened.

What just happened was that a rebellious and angry teenager, who could very well have become an ever-more-angry teenager capable of real harm, has had his rebellion embraced and redirected into something like art. If the teacher had fought him on this, the teenager would have fought harder, and would have seen this slight as yet another reason the world was an unforgiving and unlistening place. The anger of any teenage boy multiplies quickly and can exact a terrible price. Instead, the teacher, being a man of great tolerance with a writer's heart, and with a sense of humor—with acceptance instead of resistance—validated the young man's strangest notions, and the young man wrote the hell out of that bike-trip speech, and got an A minus.

He was heard. He was validated.

Okay. The teenager's next speech is about how humanity needs to beware of the coming Sheep Apocalypse—that is, a situation whereby sheep, which have been lulling us into a false sense of complacency, take over the world.

This is true. This is a true story.

Again the teacher accepts this proposal as an appropriate enough interpretation of the assignment and use of the English language, loudly implying that the interests of his students, no matter how bizarre, have to be accepted—that ideas are anarchic things, and that though the ideas can be anarchic, the form can be tamed, that even if the speech is about world-conquering sheep, if it's done well, it's valid and deserving of attention and dignity. The teenager delivers his sheep speech, laughs through half of it, but still gets an A minus.

The last speech the teenager makes that semester is not a goofy one. It is about how we need to focus on the positive. That sometimes some dark obstacle—it could be a giant spherical zit on one's nose, it could be domestic strife, it could be anything—can obscure all the good in the world. That we need to look around, and look past, these obstacles, and seek out beauty, seek out grace.

It is a corny speech. It has no edge.

But somehow in the course of the semester the young man has lost that edge, or has found a way to direct it, and because his writing has been validated by his teacher, he and a friend, a friend who also loves Monty Python (so much that this friend has adopted a British accent while living in suburban Chicago), together begin writing a column in the school newspaper called And Now for a Bit of Fun. It is absurdist and nonsensical, but they labor over every word, ten drafts, fifteen drafts, hoping that the speech teacher will like it.

This newspaper column leads to the teenager's being asked to write for the school yearbook, which he does, and working on the yearbook leads to his joining the literary magazine, which has exactly four members, who all soon graduate and cede the magazine to him and another friend, the other foot-odor friend! Together, the two young men with the school's worst foot-odor problem take over the literary magazine. Is this justice? Sign of the apocalypse? Not the sheep one, but some other, more frightening version?

In any case, between all these projects the teenager suddenly has a home. He has a tribe, and the tribe has elders. These elders are the school's English faculty, and they are held in a certain awe, because they know everything the tribe wants to know. They are a mysterious and holy sect now seen by the teenager and his literary magazine friends as their clerics and guides.

There is the literary magazine teacher–advisor, Mrs. Lowey, who is getting on in years and has trouble with stairs but who nonetheless insists on keeping her third-floor classroom because it's full of light and her paintings. She teaches the teenager everything about writing and editing fiction and poetry and introduces him to the unparalleled joy in publishing. Every day she climbs the stairs, slowly, so slowly, going higher, toward the light, and the tribe follows, and in that third-floor atelier they edit, and write, and assemble, and laugh, and feel like their tiny literary magazine is very much the center of the world and has the power to change it.

There is Mr. Benton, who has just bought and mastered the first Apple computer and laser printer, and who helps the foot-odor boys make the magazine something clean and professional, shockingly professional, and who is an opera singer on the side, and who approaches the day, every day, with the inspired glee of a true believer.

There is Mr. Hawkins, who teaches AP English, who introduces the teenager to Dostoevsky and Joseph Heller, and who is a singer-songwriter who brings down the house at every talent show.

There is Mr. Criche, the head of the English department, whom the teenager wants so badly to please that he brings a copy of *As I Lay Dying* to class every day, even though it's not required reading, hoping to impress him. Mr. Criche is not impressed by the teenager carrying around unassigned Faulkner, but he likes a paper the teenager writes about *Macbeth,* so much that he writes at the top of it, "Sure hope you become a writer." Just those six words.

This all happens just a year after the teenager has met this first teacher, Mr. Peter Ferry, and in that year just about everything changed in his life. He found his people, he found a voice, he found validation, he found purpose.

That teacher and I still show each other our work. He's usually my first reader, after my wife. And now he has published two books, too, two fantastic novels I was proud to be able to read in manuscript form.

So if you younger teachers out there think it ends when your students graduate, no such luck. They follow you around the rest of your lives. Like it or not.

I thank you teachers for what you do, and I warn you about the awesome—the original meaning of the word, which conveys a biblical power—the kind of awesome power you have. I salute you and urge you on.

Originally given as a keynote speech to the
National Council of Teachers of English national convention
in Minneapolis, Minnesota, on November 21, 2015.

The Rules

MY GOD, YOU SHOULD SEE THE LOOK of complete disappointment, of utter boredom when I tell my friends I'm writing a book about teaching. Who wants to read a book about teaching? Not even teachers. Some friends, in a heroic attempt at supportiveness, suggest ways I could try to get the book I'm writing on lists at college teacher programs. They're being sweet.

It's a fine thing when your best-case scenario is that some people may read your book, maybe, so long as it's a requirement to do so.

I'm not writing a book to sell books, though. I'm writing a book about teaching because I have some things to say about teaching. I don't know yet, but I think this book would make a great book-club book for teachers looking for yet another excuse to drink.

I'm writing this book because I often feel like I'm on an island as a teacher. I often feel like I sit through training after unhelpful training from PhDs and various people who have given up on (or never attempted) actually teaching to get to tell people how to do it right, and I feel like those people are, generally, missing the point. Usually, the icebreaker is the best part, and I genuinely, deeply hate icebreakers.

I wrote the book I wish I had when I was starting out, the book I would like to read in the times when I feel like I'm losing my way. I've been teaching a whole lot of years and have never read a whole book about teaching from cover to cover during the school year, so this book isn't designed to be read like that.

I'd read this book alone, but I don't really like people that much. I did not write it alone. I wrote it with the strength and intelligence of colleagues and friends. It grew stronger with specific input by Sarah and Jade and Brandon and Alana. I leaned heavily on Mitra and made Peter promise to finish it if I died in a plane crash. Also, there's this insane family of people who have won their state's Teacher of the Year award who have adopted me as somehow worthy, and I shudder to think where I'd be as a writer, teacher, or advocate without them.

I wrote most of this book in my head to myself ten years ago. I wrote the rest of it in early mornings at my desk, during school breaks as I could (more than three weeks removed from school and I always totally forget what teaching is like), and after my daughter went to bed.

I decided I would write a book while I was driving to Wisconsin for Christmas, and with a sleeping wife and sleeping child my only company, let my mind wander. In ten years of teaching, I've mentored many student and new teachers and found myself asking many of the same questions and telling many of the same stories, not just about teaching but what it means to be a Teacher. I thought of all of those stories, observations, and questions, everything I've learned in a decade of teaching, everything I wish someone had told me ten years ago.

As we drove, I would write in my head, then scribble down thoughts and lists and a table of contents at every bathroom and meal stop on the way. The most enduring part of those firsts lists is what follows: my rules for teaching, and my rules for writing about teaching. They are as good an introduction as I can imagine for everything else you're about to read. Or if this book has somehow made it to your book club, it will serve as enough reading to passably pretend you read everything else and try to impress your work crush.

MY RULES OF WRITING

Race is on the table.

You can't be a teacher and not think about Race. I don't care what your class looks like or what you look like, if you're talking about education and you're not talking about race, then you're not really talking about education. This book is written in the way that many teachers talk, with issues of Race, Gender, and Sexuality infused into and informing the discussions about everything else. In a job full of humans, human issues are always a priority.

No sugarcoating.

I will show you my bad days as often as my good days. I will discuss the best and worst projects, attitudes, and reactions I've gotten from students. I am on many days prouder of the best of my worsts than the best of my bests.

No research.

For my book on teaching will not be or read like a PhD thesis with a cover and quirky name slapped on the front. The loudest voices in the education of youth have white hair, PhDs, and thousands of hours of more research than I am willing to do, but none of them speaks to me. Also, sometimes I feel like data are for people who don't understand people.

I must be teaching to write about teaching.

Because I hate every staff development training that starts out, "I used to be a teacher too, but five years ago . . ." because it always sounds to me like the speaker couldn't hack it. Every right answer that I think I have about teaching and that I write all confident about will be subject to complete failure the next day in class, and will not benefit from the comfort of selective memory or a buffer of time.

The best inventions from the best systems of pedagogy, debated and constructed by the best educational brains in the country, can be thoroughly, embarrassingly, and hilariously dismantled in ten seconds by a fifteen-year-old who was just dumped by his girlfriend. If you pay attention, though, that kid is going to show you the little pieces that may be wrong in a big good idea, or may show you that some big ideas sound wonderful away from real classrooms but really have no business being there.

This is not a teaching manual, except when it is.

I'm not sure if it's possible to read something that will make you a better teacher. I think I've figured some pretty big things out, so I'm going to say some things that may help out. They will be mostly big questions to sit and think about. There won't be any activities in here that you can use for forty minutes in class fifteen minutes after you read it.

MY RULES OF TEACHING

School is unfair.

Let's imagine two students here. Both have been assigned a substantial project that requires work from home.

Student One goes home to an afternoon snack and is directed by their parents to their study space—a desk and lamp set aside just for them and their full-time job of school. The student is redirected when they lose focus and praised when they've done well. They are called to dinner, which has been made for them, and their progress is checked before free time is given, time in which they are allowed to relax, enjoy their hobbies or friends, get themselves ready for the next day.

Student Two is many different students. They have parents who work or parents who party. They have siblings to take care of or meals to make or meals that will be missed. They smoke weed for all the reasons kids do, or they date or they work. Or home is too loud, or home is unsafe, or home doesn't exist. Or they get sick when they look in the mirror or get angry for almost no reason, or they can't sit still or stay focused no matter the consequences. Maybe someone is sick, or they are, or someone every day says things to them that make school and everything related feel awful. Or for any of the whatever reasons, they aren't getting their work done tonight. When they are called out for not having their work done tomorrow, they almost surely won't say why. When they are called on it again and again and told again and again they need to show more effort, they will feel like they are already doing impossibly too much.

Also, school may be the only place where it is safe enough to laugh or quiet enough to sleep. Also, small reprimands or discouragements, small cuts at school can open deeper and older wounds.

School says that Student One is a good student, and that Student Two is a bad student. That may be true, if *student* means the ability to navigate school. Is Student One smarter, more creative, more insightful than Student Two? On a lot of days, it's really really hard to tell. Their grades would say so. That's something that's wrong with school, not something wrong with either student.

School is unimportant.

This is something I knew well when I was in school and have been slowly trained to forget during teacher education and staff meetings about chewing gum, hats, and tardies. Education is important, the ability to think in complex ways, to understand the people and the world around you, the ability to find, filter, and synthesize information is important. School is not.

Tests are unimportant. Binders and lockers, seating charts, due dates, points (oh all the talk about points), all the trappings, all the stuff of school is deeply unimportant and yet begs constant attention and energy from teachers (and often many hours of work from students).

Teachers can spend incalculable amounts of time and energy on school goals that make no sense. We imagine that our importance lies in our authority, that as gatekeepers to the pieces of paper needed to get to the next step, we have some responsibility to be harsh, punitive, or "realistic." We are preparing students for some "real world" we imagine will be best served by people who learned an important lesson by getting a D in Health and now care genuinely for people and are culturally competent critical thinkers. We worry constantly that we are not preparing our students for what they'll see in college while we push for a system that excludes many from the opportunity to try.

In three years, my students will remember very little of what I've attempted to teach them. If I'm lucky, skills will continue to transfer and build from year to year; maybe the very core of what I'm teaching will transfer and stay with them in some way. If I'm unlucky or there is a bee in the room on the wrong day, students will forget most of what I teach them. They will forget entire novels we will spend months reading only weeks after we finish reading them. They will not remember what a gerund is. They will, god forbid, forget which there/they're/their is the right one to use to show possession.

I have a year, sometimes less, to give them something useful to understand and remember. Why would we ask school to focus on anything that isn't going to be important to them?

Compassion before all else.

In my third year of teaching, just before the students came back from lunch, my whole teaching team was called to the office. Our principal delivered the news that one of our students, an eighth grade girl of profound talent and empathy, was about to be told that her mother just committed suicide. The girl's father was on the way, but we were to act as if everything was normal until he got there.

The girl was in my next class, and that hour was without a doubt the hardest I have ever had as a teacher. All these years later, I can picture where the girl was sitting, the spot behind the lab table I stood in for most of the hour. I have this weird thing where I don't connect colors to emotion, so I never remember them. I can't tell you the color of any house I've lived in, including the one I'm currently sitting in. I can't tell you the color of my classroom, or of any classroom I've ever taught in, or the color of the dress I put my daughter in this morning, or the color of a single flower, food item, or decoration at my wedding, but I remember vividly that the student was in yellow for the last hour of her life before she found out her mom was dead.

During the hour, I tried not to look at her too much, tried to act as normal as I could, tried not to break down, to run to her, to hug her and tell her a thousand times, "I'm sorry." I felt awful for knowing what I had no right to know and felt guilty for being able to teach, to joke with students, with that student in particular, knowing what I knew.

As the hour ended, she was called to the office. After twenty minutes, her three closest friends were called up as well. News spread over the next few days, and the community rallied and supported her in ways impressive and beautiful. The girl's teachers became among the most important people in her life, but not as teachers. We were people, humans, who cared for her as a person. What she needed, the only thing she needed, for the last few months of school, was as much humanity and care and support as we could give her, and so we did, because more than teacher and students, she was a human and we were all humans.

Teaching is completely full of humans.

Really, full of them. Real humans. Oh, and how often we forget. Oh, and how much did any training, education, staff development, or research about teaching get me ready for my most trying moments, for that or any other of the many times I've felt the most effective and important and influential at my job? Not at all. Because Teaching is only sometimes about teaching. Teachers are far too often complaining about not getting to do their jobs because they don't get enough time just saying things for kids to write down. Teaching is so rarely that, is more often about doing all the work to get a student to that moment, is more often supporting a kid who is far away from being taught that day.

I am not an expert teacher. My ten full years feel plenty long to me but are eclipsed by triple by at least a few people in my building. They are experts. I have a master's degree in English Education, but, if I'm honest, I didn't really work all that hard at it. So, I promise no answers.

In the short time I've been doing this, I have learned that anyone promising answers to teaching is almost surely full of shit. I have my answers, and I'm sure I'll end up sharing everything I think I've learned, but my answers work for me, in the building I work, and with the students I have. If there were one method of instruction, assessment, or classroom management that worked well for everyone, then teaching would be ridiculously easy, and we'd all be a lot better at it.

Anyone who's done it for longer than a day knows that teaching is messy business. Each school is different, and each classroom for that matter, and each group of students, and each kid is different, and every kid is different on different days, or by different friends, or doing different sorts of things. Messy, messy, messy.

I've found that applying a system broadly, any system, no matter how well engineered or well intentioned or well researched, means you miss kids and means kids miss opportunities. This is the problem with most books, manuals, and teacher education classes. They skip to the final step and don't spend nearly long enough on the core reasons why we do what we do. So often while I got my license I heard professors say, "We're all here for the right reasons." So often in staff meetings now I hear, "We all want the same thing for students," and then we jump to how we get to that thing.

We don't talk about the reasons. We don't spend time on the questions that created the answers in the first place.

We really like to talk about strategies. In interviews, we love teachers with great answers about classroom management strategies. We love to talk about grading strategies, how to put desks where, how to stand or sit when talking to students in which situations. When we're done with strategies, we talk about policies.

I hereby suggest that all strategies are either equally bullshit or equally valuable. What we do is far less important than why we do it. All the carefully implemented management strategies won't matter for shit if you don't know your kids and they don't know you care about them. Answers don't make good teachers, questions do. This simple statement took me every moment of the first six and a half years of my teaching to really understand.

I read a lot about teaching when I was in school to be a teacher. We talked all the time about all the different things we would need. We talked so often about strategies. Strategies were named, then acronymed, taken as notes, discussed as theoreticals. Never once was there a strategy introduced for what to do when a student finds out in the middle of your class that their mother has died tragically. Any strategy presented anywhere would be wrong anyway. Besides, it was an intense day, the hardest day I've ever had as a teacher, but is one of only about a hundred different times I've had a student in crisis in front of me. Sometimes they wear those crises like fire, they scream and they spread and they destroy. Sometimes they wear those crises like Frodo wore the ring, secretly, around their necks, weighing them down. Is it inappropriate to make a *Lord of the Rings* reference regarding students in crisis? It is.

There is no right way to treat those kids, no strategy that makes their parent's death not hurt, that makes their home suddenly safe, that makes their addiction disappear. We can be kind, we can care.

That student, those students, is the reason this book is full of questions. You may have one group figured out in May, but you'll get a new group in September and you'll learn, because we all learn, that what worked last year won't work this year. Each year's class is a whole new group of humans complete with all the mess of humans. Their lives are not static, so we can't be static. We can ask the same questions every year, the questions that have given us success, the questions that have helped us help kids, but we can't expect the same answers, can't assume the answers will be the same without asking. Teaching is hard, and one of the hardest things about it is that it never gets easy. Welcome to the shit show.

Part I

SUMMER

In summer, we reflect on the year we had and have weird worry dreams about the year on the way.

We find jobs and prepare, mentally and physically.

Also, we sometimes drink at noon outside on a beautiful day when all our sucker friends are working in offices.

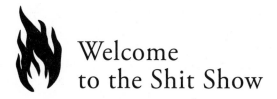

Welcome
to the Shit Show

ALL OF THE SOON-TO-BE-QUESTIONED CHOICES in your life have led to this moment. You are standing in front of a group of students you are supposed to teach. Okay. Now what?

You wanna know what's gonna happen? Total ridiculousness. All the time. If you don't have teacher friends, get teacher friends, because no one else will understand or believe the stories that you will bring home. There will be a point when your day will contain a handful of crying kids, a few legitimate crises, a level of in-fighting and pettiness among staff members that would make middle school mean girls blush, and at least one moment when you are working with a student, your head in your hands, pleading desperately for them to either just put their name on a thing that will keep them from failing, or to stop, pretty please stop, putting that thing inside their ear (it will get stuck there, and only an ER visit will remedy the situation). When someone asks you what happened at work that day, you will respond, "Nothing, really," because that will be a pretty normal and unremarkable day.

Welcome to the shit show.

I mean it, really. Welcome. We're glad to have you and in fact really need you. I also mean it, really mean it, that schools are a shit show. Every one of them, nearly all the time, for a million different reasons.

Very early in my first year, really, like two weeks in at most, I was out in the hallway checking on a group. We were doing *Romeo and Juliet* and the kids were all doing two-minute movies of each act so we could compile a ten-minute version of the play and get all that plot garbage out of the way, because if you're teaching Shakespeare to study his broke-ass stolen plots and not the language, well, then, you, sir, are no friend of mine.

But. Yeah. I was out talking to the group doing the third act (which includes all sorts of great Mercutio stuff, including his death, which is that huge moment where the play flips from a comedy to a tragedy but in this case meant a lot of kids with nerf swords banging the hell out of each other in a conference room and needing at least a little supervision). I was out of my room for maybe two minutes, and when I came back in, there was a large table flipped over and a silence that could only have meant that I missed something big.

At first the students in the class were holding steady to the story that no one flipped the table.

ME: Was it flipped before?
STUDENTS: No.
ME: Is it flipped now?
STUDENTS: Yes.
ME: So what happened?
STUDENTS: Nothing.
ME: Get back to work.

Ten minutes later, after asking questions of the scared kids who I knew would tell me everything (and did), it turned out that two students who are always bickering started straight up fighting. Ben, who hates Victoria and loves her, was being ruthless to Victoria. Victoria, who hates Ben and loves him, had had too much and launched at Ben, wrapping her hands around his throat and sending them both over a table. So that was a thing that happened that day.

I brought Ben and Victoria together into the hallway.

ME: What happened?
THEM: Nothing.
ME: Nothing? Did someone get choked?
THEM: Yes.
ME: Did you both fly over a table and knock it over?
THEM: Yes.
ME: So what happened?
THEM: Nothing.

Just two kids, you know, doing what kids do, you know. Just a little choking and some tackling, but pretty much nothing. They really weren't trying to get out of trouble. They were actually pretty surprised that it was something they could get in trouble for. Through all my work, through an arduous and unseemly process of licensure and untold hours writing essays about research I didn't really read, I had asked to be there in that moment.

And on that same day, on that same goddamn day, in the middle of another class, a girl reached straight down the front of her shirt and pulled a penny from her bra. Another student sitting close by saw the whole thing happen and went "EWWW!" in the way that middle school kids do when confronted with things that are different and things that involve bras. The girl turned to the boy and, exercising really her only option at that point, threw the penny at the boy and hit him in the leg.

I have no idea what she had that penny for, or why it was in her bra, or why that moment was the moment that she just had to have it out of her bra, but okay. The bra penny had been cast and hit the kid with really no force at all (except the cosmic weight of a penny that had just been removed from someone's shirt).

So the boy, this kid, did what he felt was the only proper response. He screamed, he wailed. He professed, again and again, that his leg had been killed. When he walked, he did so dragging his leg behind him, lifeless. He did this through the rest of the class, and then on the way to lunch, during recess, and, yes, all through games of volleyball at gym. I talked to him about it.

Every adult all day talked to him about it, first pleading and then demanding that he stop pretending his leg was dead.

I distinctly remember, and this was a moment I had worked my ass off for years to be in, work that I had gone into deep debt to get the chance to do, a job that I had literally, actually, assassinated three competitors to have, and I remember sitting with this kid after a few hours of his dragging around his leg behind him in the hallway and telling him, "I understand you didn't want a bra penny thrown at you, but acting like that penny killed your leg is really pretty offensive."

"I'm not acting," he replied. "It's really dead. The penny killed it." (This is not the weirdest conversation I've had with a student.) And he dragged his leg off to math. A not-small part of me was impressed with his commitment to the bit.

One more from my first year: there was this kid Ian with long straight hair he was constantly flipping out of his eyes, jeans that cost more than my car, and the sort of pudgy confidence that comes with being from an especially wealthy family. "I don't have to work in school," he once told me, "because I'm already smarter than most people, and I'm just going to have a job at my dad's company anyway." Okay.

The thing about Ian is that, all that aside, he was generally an okay kid so long as no one was suggesting that it wasn't okay for him to be the center of the world at all times. For example, he excelled at giving presentations but was absolutely god-awful when it was time for someone else to speak. Just before winter break, we were doing just such a thing, each student presenting to the class on three different dialects used in their lives. Ian sat near the back, and I sat near Ian, hoping my proximity would keep him from bothering each and every presenter. He did, for the most part, leave them alone, but only because he spent the entire hour turned sideways in his chair, looking right at me, trying to have a conversation with me while I tried to focus on the front of the room.

"Have you ever been a vegetarian?" "What do you think shark tastes like?" "How many people do you think it would take to lift a car off the ground?" "What's your favorite country?"

Question after inane question went unanswered. I thought, I hoped, that ignoring him would possibly make him give up. Actually, I didn't really think it would help, but I was curious what would happen if I gave him absolutely zero of the attention he was asking for.

"Hey, guess what?" Nothing. "Guess what I can do?" Staring forward. "I can fit my hand in my mouth." Nope, not responding, just grading presentations.

And then he was screaming. Well, he was screaming as well as he could with his hand in his mouth.

Yep. It had gotten stuck there. His entire fucking hand, stuck in his mouth.

TEACHING IS A SHIT SHOW, and that shit show really hits you during the beginning of your career, during the beginning of every year, the end of every year, when you start at a new school, and for any chunk of days before or after a break or long weekend. Yes, that leaves, like, three days of the year that are pretty chill (teachers say, "This is a hard part of the year" about every part of the year but summer). Believe me, I know, because though all these stories so far have been from my first year of teaching, I am now in my tenth, and though I really kinda feel like I know what I'm doing, I'm trying to do those things in a new building, and I am getting my ass handed to me.

I am now that teacher who will ask a student to get to class, please and please, again and again, and be ignored (when I'm lucky and not told off for getting all in someone's business), until another teacher walks by and says, "Class," and off the student will go. I was that teacher last year, the teacher who could move the unmovable child, who could pipe in, obnoxiously, in meetings for a student removing bricks of the school one at a time, about how well that student was doing in my class, and, hey, here's an example of a cool project they did for me. Oh, they glued all your desks to the wall while you turned around for three seconds? Weird. That hasn't happened in my room. I was that teacher last year, and this year I'm spending as much time scrubbing "bitch" or "deez nutz" (somehow, again, a thing) off a wall as I am doing my actual, real job.

A lot of the time, it just takes a lot of time.

A lot of the time, it takes standing in front of a student and taking their worst and coming back the next day, because they are trying to scare you away. The broken of my new school has very little in common with the broken I left, so I need to learn this new broken better. There are simple things you can do, and they mostly mean spending time now to make things easier later. Going to lunch or recess, or hanging with your kids in art, or talking to them like real-life people who are, somehow, for the first time ever in humanity, struggling with adolescence.

The most important thing to do is understand the insanity, embrace the shit show, but don't let it become you. I've seen too many teachers act in school like they are back in school. They track student relationships and friendships. They spend hours navigating the interpersonal drama of students, things that are very little of their business and ultimately are important for kids to figure out by themselves. Those teachers often spend an equal number of hours on the rumors and power struggles on staff, a game of who said what to whom that a good many of us were happy to leave behind in seventh grade.

When you are surrounded by drama and downright ridiculousness, it's hard not to see those things as a legitimate way to work, but they are not. Your job as a grown-ass person in a school building is to act like one, ride the insanity as often as you can, ignore it when you can't, and drink at night when neither of those things works.

The other day, I was helping out with recess, trying to wrangle kids who would rather not be wrangled just before a long weekend. It was time for the middle school to be out there, so I was surprised to see a rather large group of elementary students run from the small wooded area a little more than ten minutes after their recess was supposed to be over. I barked at them and pointed, not generally that interested in getting too close to kids that small, but they bee-lined for me anyway.

"There's a body back there!"

"Go to . . ." *Wait, a fuckwhatnow?* ". . . a what?"

"There's a body! Tylersaidhesawabodyandwewentandlooked" (*deep breath*) "andIsawitsfaceandAngelasawitsfingers" (*deep breath*) "soitsabodyanditsbackinthewoodsandwehadtogoseeit!"

Umm. Yeah. Okay.

So I got them to head back toward the building and started walking, I guess, to go and find the body. That's what I was doing with my day, at that point. Lesson plan, sure. Do attendance, grade some papers, all that makes sense for a teacher to do. Go find a body in the woods? Yeah, that's got to be in the job description somewhere.

The little wooded area was creepy as hell, a truly random assortment of the kinds of things people throw into a wooded area that kind of doesn't belong to anyone. Under no circumstances, of course, were kids supposed to go back here during recess, which means they nearly always do. I spent about ten minutes just looking around all the crap. I was being quiet, you know, so as not to warn the dead body I was coming in case it tried to get me.

There was a giant broken flat-screen TV, three shopping carts belonging to stores that were all at least five miles away, and a crappy old sleeping bag that, when looked at just right kinda, I guess, looked like it could be a body. It wasn't. I mean, I wasn't going to go nudge it with my foot or anything to make sure, but it wasn't. Nobody there. No body there.

My principals were in a meeting that I had to pull them from, and I got to start a conversation with, "Okay . . . so just know that there isn't a body in the woods." It took about an hour of walking from room to room, and then the social worker going to check, and then the school cop guy going to check before just about all the students stopped spreading the rumor that there was a body in the woods. Turns out it was probably a ghost.

This all happened right around lunchtime, and by the time I got home and my wife asked me how my day was, I answered, "Pretty good. Pretty normal." Only during the next day when we were watching the news did I remember, "Oh yeah, yesterday I was pretty sure I was about to find a dead person at work, but I didn't."

"How did you not lead with that when you walked in the door?"

"Forgot."

Hey, you know what? This will be your life. This and so many more things will be the constant experience of being you as long as you have this job. But here's the thing, and the thing that will maybe help you at some point: it's not just your kids, it's not just your school. Kids are weird, teachers are weirder, and when you smash them all together for a hundred-whatever days a year, really weird things happen. Some of those weird things are brilliant, some of them are downright terrible, but none of them will happen only at your school, only in your room, only because of you. You asked for this, but you're not alone.

The Interview

I STUDENT-TAUGHT IN A HIGH SCHOOL where students were patted down and walked through metal detectors every morning. I went to a high school in an affluent suburb in Wisconsin. My school was one of the top schools in the state in college acceptance and featured shockingly great facilities for theater, athletics, and certain kinds of music. In my high school, hats were banned for fear they might be used as a way to signal gang affiliations. That term, *gang affiliations,* was said in whispers. The worry that a gang would somehow infiltrate a school that had snowmobile parking in the winter, that students would become spontaneously infected by gangyness, that the infection would spread through hat wearing, was a tangible fear our administration carried around in their front pockets.

When I student-taught, hats were still banned but almost constantly worn. No one worried much about the hats showing gang affiliation, because no one was trying very hard to hide their gang affiliations. Most actual gang activity happened just off of school grounds, but occasionally friction from outside the building found its way in. One time, a group of kids who were not students at the school kicked their way in through a side door to jump someone in the hallway.

Another time, two groups fought in the hallway right in front of our classroom. My co-operating teacher, seven months pregnant and ten times the badass I will ever be, was running into the fray to pull out one student who would be in danger of expulsion if he was caught fighting again. I stopped her, and we made a quick decision that she would hold our kids in the room while I attempted to grab our student from the mob. Just as I reached the group, the police officer assigned to the building reached the top of the stairs and pepper-sprayed the whole group, me included. I had never found occasion to be pepper-sprayed before that moment, so it was a novel experience for me. Snot came out of my nose, mouth, and eyeballs. It wasn't pleasant.

Although the event was among the more memorable experiences of my student teaching, it wasn't really indicative of the larger experience. I loved the school, the teachers in the school, and, most especially, the students there. I learned many, many things that kept me from completely bursting into flames in my first year, and many things that helped me in the interview that eventually got me the job I still hold.

The day of my job interview started with fossils.

I originally wasn't going to go on the field trip. I thought about taking the morning off to rest up and rehearse god-knows-what before heading into my first teaching interview. But then the day before the trip there was a planning meeting, and the teaching team decided that though most students would be grouped into their first-hour classes, there was a group of six or seven kids with particular problems in the area of self-control that could use a smaller group. The problem, of course, was finding a staff person who would be in charge of that group.

I had a good relationship with many of the students (who were all in an afternoon class I taught called "Literacy," which was meant for students more than two grade levels behind in reading who did not qualify for special ed. In other words, kids who had been screwed by more than a few parts of life and who we couldn't seem to stop screwing), so I was volunteered. "It won't be a problem," my cooperating teacher told me, "because we'll be back at school an hour before your interview, which will be plenty of time." Of course.

It rained all night and some of the morning, but why would

that stop us? The buses were ordered! It stopped raining, just, by the time the buses got to the park where we would, if there was a god, find a fucking trilobite. I do not remember if we found one or not. I know at one point we saw a frog and it scared the living shit out of one of the kids, a seventeen-year-old girl who had never seen a real frog before. I also know there was mud, and that under that mud there was more muddier mud. In some places, there was gravelly stuff that was unlikely to yield sciencey finds but looked less muddy and so was where we focused our efforts (though we quickly found that under the gravelly stuff was just gravelly muddy mud).

Mud, or poor planning, or both meant that we did not finish up and get back on the bus until right about the time that we were supposed to be back at school. Drumming nervously on the green vinyl seat in front of me did not help our bus get us to the school any faster than twenty minutes before my interview. The second floor boy's bathroom of a high school isn't the best place to feel professional, but I did my best to wipe the mud from my face and neck down to my chest, and from my hands up to my wrists. A suit was applied carefully over the mud covering the rest of my body, and I was off to try to convince a group of people to put me in charge of the future of our nation.

On the way over, I promised myself I would not show anyone the mud. I tried many hand gestures and sitting postures to make sure the shirt would not slide up or down in a way that would show that most of my body remained completely covered. I got lost on the way to the school, and then couldn't find the door, and then got into the school and got lost in the school.

A teacher found me standing in the hallway, turning in circles looking for . . . something? They asked if they could help, and I explained to them I was on a field trip all day and was now late to an interview in this building somewhere. Ah. And where was the office? By the front door. Where was the front door? By the front of the school. Of course. I totally could have thought of that by myself if not for the trilobites. I managed to be just barely on time, if not a bit frantic.

I was led to a conference room with an already-sitting interview committee. They looked a lot like a room full of people who had been interviewing dicks like me all day long. They did not light up upon seeing that I held many copies of my portfolio. They did appreciate the much shorter collection of "best of's" that could be flipped through in five minutes and that had little stickers on every page explaining what each was and why. That, there, was an actually helpful piece of advice for interviewing: make one of those. No one wants to look at your whole damn portfolio.

Everyone introduced themselves, and then we sat quiet.

The silence seemed like a tricky interview trick.

"Am I supposed to start?"

"No, the principal isn't here yet. We just have to wait." It wasn't a tricky trick.

"Oh." More quiet. "So, my arms are totally full of mud right now." I'm not good at shutting up.

Suddenly I was talking about trilobites and mud and buses and getting lost. I was also rolling up my shirtsleeves to show them just how filthy I was under my suit. My legs, I promised, were similarly muddy, but I did not (thank god) lift them above the table to prove my point.

So I broke my rule about the mud pretty early on. Telling the story gave me a chance to humble-brag about being chosen to be with the group of troublesome kids. Showing off my mud like a war wound won me some points with the science teacher.

Eventually, the principal made it in after handling a bus issue, and the interview began. Each member of the interview committee (three teachers I would be working closely with, the principal, the director of HR, and her assistant) had a sheet in front of them of interview questions. The group went around the table, each reading a question in turn. I passed around my best-of sheet, and everyone flipped through it when it wasn't their turn to ask a question. My portfolio, probably a hundred sheets of papers, lesson plans, and everything else I had worked the past year and a half to compile, sat unopened on the table.

There were many questions, maybe twenty, but I remember a few clearly now and remember my answers pretty well. So here's my interview, as best as I can remember, and removing what I'm sure were plenty of instances of "Hmm, well, umm, let me think . . ." Oh, and I should point out that the principal came in, sat in the back corner, and looked almost immediately like he had fallen asleep. He did not read questions. So I was pretty sure from the outset that I was screwed and ended up answering honestly and emotionally instead of trying to guess what they wanted to hear.

[Also, I'm going to throw in hints, like this, in case you're planning for your own interviews.]

> GLASSES MATH TEACHER: What do you think your
>   biggest strengths are as a teacher?
> ME: My flexibility, and my creativity. The other day
>   there was an all-school assembly that wasn't an-
>   nounced until the school day had already begun. It
>   was supposed to last the entirety of my fifth hour,
>   but it only lasted half the hour, so I suddenly went
>   from having an hour-long lesson planned to think-
>   ing I would do none, to suddenly having about a
>   half-hour with kids who were completely wound up
>   from having their day interrupted. So I knew my
>   other lesson wouldn't work and I didn't want to give
>   them free time or study hall or anything, so I quick-
>   ly came up with a little creative writing thing we
>   could all do together. It was high-energy and social,
>   and we had a really good time with it.

[*Note*: Tell stories when you can. Narratives about your teaching make you a person and give you a chance to explain who you really are as a teacher. Do that.]

> SPIKY-HAIRED SOCIAL STUDIES TEACHER: What is
>   something you would change about education if
>   you could?
> ME: I have this student right now, and from the first

day I've met him, he's said that he wants to be a rapper. It's just about the only thing he cares about, just about the only thing he will work at, only he's scared of performing. I've noticed, and I don't mean to call other teachers out, but I've noticed that when a lot of teachers talk to this student, or about this student, they talk about all the things that are like rap that he could do. He could be a sound engineer, or a promoter, or could go into production of some sort. It's like they're applying this middle-class White lens about what success is to what the student is saying, instead of just listening to what the kid is saying. So I work with him on stage fright, talk about when I was nervous performing and what I would do, and I encourage his rapping. So that didn't totally answer the question, except for that kid, but the thing teachers are doing to that kid is happening all over schools. We are applying our own standards of success, or what sorts of jobs or lives are acceptable or desirable, to the kids we have instead of listening to what they really want.

[*Note*: More stories! Also, the principal looked like he woke up a little at this one, and then just looked sort of angry, or maybe hungry, and then looked like he fell asleep again. He may also have just been staring at his phone. Also, most schools are looking for teachers who care enough about the profession to have ideas about the profession. Look for questions like this.]

ACTUAL GLITTER MAKEUP ON SCIENCE TEACHER: Tell us about a time that you were challenged as a teacher, and what you did to meet that challenge.

ME: Well, okay. This just happened a few weeks ago now. There's a student I have now, and his name is Jordan. Jordan can be pretty hard to engage in school but is generally pretty interested in talking. The other day he came in just completely shut down, obviously upset. I let him alone during class, because honestly he just looked violently angry, and I was worried about pushing him at all. When class ended he just sat there as the other kids emptied out, just sat there and stared down at his desk. It was my prep hour, so it was just the two of us, and I went and sat by him, just sat quiet for a few minutes, and then he just started letting everything out. The night before, his older brother had been shot and killed. Someone was mad at him and shot him in the chest with a shotgun, and he had died immediately.

So I grew up in an all-White suburb in Wisconsin, and here's this kid just breaking down in front of me, and his brother has been shot. And you know? They don't cover that stuff in education classes.

So I just listened. I don't know why, but it seemed like more than anything it would be good to walk, but I didn't want to walk around the hallways where everyone would see him crying and want to ask him about stuff, so we walked outside. I also didn't want to leave school property, so we just walked the block of the school. We probably did the lap ten times over the hour, and he just talked and I just listened. We went back inside before the next class started, and he gave a really quick "K, thanks," and walked down the hall.

I have no idea if I did the right thing or did anything, but it was the thing I did.

[*Note*: You don't need a huge tragedy to answer this question, but you do need honesty. Almost certainly, the people in the room of your interview will know what teaching is like, and an answer about how you just work too hard and teach too perfect won't fly. Every day is full of legitimate challenges, admit it. How you handle them is the important part.]

MATH-MATH GLASSES TEACHER (whom I didn't know
yet but who would turn out to be the absolute best
teacher I've ever worked with [sorry, all those other
teachers]): Do you have any questions for us?
ME: What is your school like for the kids who go here?

[*Note*: I pulled this question out of my ass but was told later
it was the moment that secured the job for me for most of the
room. Most people use this question to ask about benefits, salary, work hours, and a million other things about them. I used it
to ask about the student experience, and I gave the people in the
room a chance to talk about the things in their school they were
the most proud of without asking them directly. They loved it.
Steal this.]

The interview ended and everyone stood up to shake my
hand, except the principal, who appeared to now be checking his
email and gave me a little wave on my way out. I learned later
that I was the last interview of the day, and when I left everyone
sat down to talk over the candidates. Before the conversation
could begin, the principal stopped everyone and said, "It's obvious, right?"

The next day as I was walking out of school, I got a call.

"Hello, this is HR-person calling to let you know that we'd
like to offer you the job you interviewed for yesterday."

"Really?"

"Yes. If you have some questions for me, I'd be glad to answer them. Otherwise, if you need some time, I can give you my
number so you can call me back with your answer."

"Really?"

"Yes, Mr. Rademacher, you're the first choice and the first
person we've called. The principal asked that we call your ref-
erences today so we could offer you the job as soon as possible.
I'm sure you have some questions about salary and benefits, and
if you'd like to schedule a meeting with me before you make
your decision, I'd be glad to make time for you in the next day
or two."

"Really?"

"Really."

So I had my first teaching job, and it would be a decade before I applied for another. I credit getting and loving my job in the district with my honesty in the interview. When I look back on it, if I wasn't such a cocky ass, or if I hadn't assumed it was a losing cause anyway, I wouldn't have called out schools on systemic racism. I wouldn't have admitted taking a student for a walk in the middle of the school day, and I certainly wouldn't have flaunted muddy arms to a table of strangers. Ultimately, though, I wouldn't have been happy at a school that wouldn't want me to do those things.

Job hunting can feel desperate, and can legitimately be desperate, but an interview is a chance to get to know a school as much as it is a chance for the school to know you. Come with questions, come with ideas of what you're looking for in a teaching environment. It may be that the perfect place isn't there for you right away, but that doesn't mean you should settle for a place you will hate.

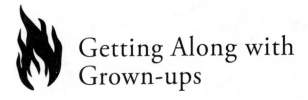

Getting Along with Grown-ups

IT IS JUNE 28, which is almost July. Almost July, and I am on vacation with my daughter. My mom owns a small condo on a large river, and because grandmas can't say no to grandchildren, I have slept an hour longer than my daughter (I cannot call it "sleeping in" when anyone without children is still asleep). My mom and daughter are outside by the river, tossing bread to squirrels, because this is apparently a thing people do here (it should be noted that "here," in this case, is Wisconsin, but maybe that's obvious, what with the whole bread/squirrels thing). Birds are chirping sweetly, the sun is painting a picture of abstract beauty and profound power across the water. I am drinking instant coffee that, paired with the taste of yesterday's sunblock on my lips, tastes like camping. Occasionally, a woodpecker hops by (at least, I've identified the strange-looking bird as a woodpecker because of its remarkable similarity to Woody). All of this is true. It is obviously, almost obnoxiously, summer.

Except my shoulders hurt wildly, hurt in the way they do when I am stressed about school, which I am. This is because for the past three hours of sleep, the only three continuous hours granted me by my daughter (back from squirrels and currently holding my phone and dancing to LMFAO in the middle of the room, slightly diminishing the feeling of my perfect and still summer morning), I dreamt about day after day of school. I had meetings that were demeaning and passive aggressive.

You see, my school, award winning and consistently gaining national and international attention, is run completely wrong. It's run so wrong that people are quitting, giving up midyear; so wrong that last summer numerous people were hired for new jobs and quit before they started because they were scared off by the way we do things; so wrong that while the morning shifts from sunned to sunny, and my daughter is already wearing her swimsuit in anticipation of a water park we are going to in four hours, my shoulders hurt from a meeting in a dream, and nearly everyone I work with would understand why.

One major problem in my school is that, fairly often, we are awful to each other. I'll get back to bosses, but before you deal with them, you need to deal with whoever works next door, and the neighbors in my neighborhood have been acting a damn fool. There's infighting, as there would be with any organization, but my god, I swear there's a vicious life-or-death flavor to it that is incredibly unnecessary.

It's also supercomplicated. So bear with me here while I try to sketch it out.

Teacher A is newer to the school, only in their third year. Their arrival on the floor was heralded by admin at first, but they have now been branded a "troublemaker" by Teacher B, and likely by Administrators A and B. Teacher A has an alliance with Teachers C, D, and E that is friendly and involves lunches with laughing and knowledge of partners' names and careers. Teacher A has an alliance with Teachers F and G that is tenuous at best and formed mainly around their mutual dislike of Teachers H and I. Oh my god, Teacher I: almost the whole floor can't even begin to stand Teacher I. Teachers F and G use words like *hate* toward Teacher I. They also use words like *fascist* and *oppression* to describe Teacher I and Teacher I's relationship with Administrator B. Teacher I lives on an island in a sea of teachers who will not talk to or recognize the existence of a real-live Person I. You could draw a map of all that, but that map would just say "second floor," and we've got three more floors after that.

Oh, but here's the thing. Teacher C doesn't actually like Teacher A and spreads rumors about Teacher A sleeping with Education Assistant A and Arts Teacher A. Teacher B thinks everyone is sleeping with everyone, or trying to, and also thinks all other teachers are whiny jerks.

This is just the beginning. Really. It gets a whole lot seedier from there. People wish harm on each other, say "Maybe they'll get hit by a car" when they walk down the street. In fact, I think I said that once. I know I said that once. I said that recently about Teacher S. You see, though I really have no emotional attachment to any of the teachers represented throughout the alphabet of teachers above, I hate S, and that big shiny S stands for Superman.

Superman is not, you will not be surprised, the person's name, nor is it a representation of that person's ability. Superman is Superman only in all the ways that Superman is the doucheyest of all superheroes and probably a total bummer to hang out with. I hate Superman, and it's ridiculous that I do. Superman never did anything to me. He's met my wife, child, and dog and did not punch any one of them in the face. He's never stolen from me, spit on me, or, to be honest, been anything other than mildly unpleasant to me. I just hate his stupid face and his stupid hair and his stupid way that he says stupid things.

I'm wrong.

Whenever you sound like a five-year-old describing your relationship with another human being, you are wrong, and it's time for you to stop being wrong.

One thing that Superman does wrong, and something that contributes to my hatred of him, and one thing that the alliances and battles serve is that he believes that anything we do at school can be done by ourselves, so he doesn't need anyone else. Wrong.

Wrong, wrong, wrong. Why? Because kids walk out of your room and into others; because kids can feel dysfunction before they get off the bus in the morning; because kids deserve the efforts of everyone working together instead of everyone working alone; because kids deserve teachers who other teachers can question and critique and inform and support. Here's my hard-won bit of wisdom, developed after a few years of watching my talent as a lecturer and curriculum developer count for much less than I thought it would: if you're going to be good at this, you're not going to do it alone.

So I get frustrated with Superman, carry that frustration around like a brick, like a brick on a rope around my neck, hanging backwards. Then, every few months, I pull my head out of my ass and I walk up to him and say something well rehearsed and insightful. Usually it's something like "Hey." Then he says, "Hey." And then, whatever. We're fine for a while.

We are two incredibly difficult White men with two incredibly huge White-man egos, but both of us are able to recognize that this whole thing we're doing is more important than that. Work is too silly to get into fights about. Teaching is too important to let dumb things like someone's stupid spiky hair get in the way, especially someone who also cares deeply about kids and has neat thoughts and lots of energy to make things better.

After lesson plans and grading and special ed meetings and pulling that kid aside at the end of the day who said that thing that you were pretty sure meant he wanted to do something impossible and illegal to half the women in the world, but whose slang, when translated, revealed something about how *wet* means "cool," and *shoes* meant "shoes," and so actually he was just talking about going shopping. After all that, I have about three and a half minutes to try to fix any problems in the school that are not things literally on fire (smoldering will be ignored). That means a whole heck of a lot of leadership (and by *leadership* I mean "rumors") happens outside of the school day. This is time I could be with my family, or not with my family, or whatever. So is it worth spending time during actual real-person time trying to plot the destruction of Superman? No. Superman is a dweeb, but Lex Luthor is an asshole.

It's all about priorities. In the time that we have, we can try to fix maybe the top three problems in a school building over the course of a year. If we can forget the smaller problems as often as possible, we have a better chance of fixing the big ones. Knowing so helps me listen to a lot of dumb shit from people I don't like because I know I don't have to fix whatever it is, not until we're about eighty problems down the list. Besides, the other great thing about focusing on big problems is that the big problems are often the ones everyone agrees on, even the dumb people I don't like. So sure, Superman, I don't think your work Facebook picture should be one of you with your shirt off, but let's sit and talk about increasing involvement in our arts opportunities. Let's make something happen.

Then again, I woke up this morning so stressed by work stuff that didn't even happen that I couldn't relax watching a river at nearly dawn. So it's hard to pretend I'm a master of not letting stuff get to me, but here's the thing—the thing big enough it gets its own paragraph, maybe extra space around this paragraph so it sticks out on the page:

It's work. It's just work. The worst thing anyone can do to you is fire you. That's it. If you start to hear people use words like *oppression* or compare your workplace to Soviet-era Russia with regards to e-mail etiquette or bus duty, and especially if you hear all those things in the same five minutes of one union meeting, it's time to start remembering that somewhere sometime soon there will be actual kids counting on you to be grown-ups and give them tools for their real lives.

Which isn't to say that it doesn't get bad, and it isn't to say that it doesn't get hard. It's just work, sure, but it's also your profession, and it's the place and the thing that you spend more time and energy on than all the other things in your life combined. So when you get yelled at or treated poorly, it stings.

When I was a first-year teacher, there was a situation at another school in our district. A teacher, talking to his elementary class, answered a question honestly about who lived in his home. See, he was a man and he lived with his partner, who was a man, and he didn't lie to his kids about this very human thing. He sent a letter home that day with his students letting their parents know that the conversation came up and that some kids may have questions. No biggie. Like, actually, not even a decade later, this is not even a thing anymore. During that year, though, just a few days later, there were protestors outside the building and news articles and a pile and a half of ridiculous.

The district stood behind the teacher, and I wanted to as well. I talked to my students about it, and two students wrote a letter to the editor of the paper. That letter got sent from my work e-mail, and suddenly I was being called to the office. In my school, there were two ways to be called to the office. There was the call asking when you had a moment ("Could you please come up?"), and then there was Kathy. Kathy was a licensed teacher who ran our after-school program but was free from school duties during large parts of the day. Sometimes, they just sent Kathy to watch your class with a message that you were wanted upstairs right now. This was never, ever a good thing. So it was a Kathy day.

My assistant principal yelled at me for a while. Yelled. Out loud. Adult to adult, presumably, and professional to profession-al, I suppose. I was called to the principal's office and yelled at. When she was done, she got the principal on the phone. He was at the hospital, as his first child had been born the day before. He, from the hallway outside of the room of his day-old off-spring, yelled at me some more. I shouldn't have sent anything from school e-mail. Check.

I know I'm not a reliable source here, but I promise, I prom-ise you, it wasn't that big of a deal.

I was sent back to my room. I was told the superintendent would be notified, and that the superintendent would likely be talking to me soon. So it was a crying day. That was a day of stomach-removal badness. At a certain point, I was sitting in my room, staring at a wall, wondering if I should wait to get fired or go upstairs and quit. The assistant principal (AP) walked into my room looking rather somber.

"I talked to the superintendent."

" . . . " I wasn't in the mood to talk anymore, and when I get really angry, I get silent.

"He said that I should come down and apologize." [*Record-scratch sound.*] "He said I should tell you that your job is safe, your intentions should be applauded, and that I should come down and tell you that, because you were probably feeling like you just got your butt kicked." [*Record exploding into a billion pieces sound.*]

"I was." I was.

This, administrator friends (if I had any), is how you get loyal-ass employees. There were many situations over the following six years that it would have been beneficial to me, or at least far easier for me, to jump on the pile of people saying bad things about the superintendent when some of his shit hit the fan. But, nope, I had his back. I had his back, and just happened in those six years to find myself in a leadership position where my having his back meant something. Not just because he helped me out, not just because he didn't yell at me, but because he treated me like a real-live person on a day that no one else did.

Hey. Be a person who does that.

When I was a fifth-year teacher, I was a man of big ideas and boundless energy. I was having a masterpiece year. I was having my *Black Album* year. I won some awards; I had multiple programs I was working on included in building tours; I had an AP who would come to me to ask for approval for things happening in the building, and a supportive principal who would sign off on most any idea I sent his way. Above all that, I worked with a team of teachers that, given three years, five thousand dollars, and a white board, could have fixed all of education everywhere. Things were so very good.

We called ourselves "The Family" (because we saw each other way more than we saw our actual families), and we were all entirely different from one another, In fact, we worked because we were all entirely different from one another.

Our Math teacher Kristen was organized, well researched, and pulled every stupid conversation we tried to have back to what was best right now for the kids in our room. She kept us grounded and focused on our work as an expression of care. She taught math with a patience, talent, and calm that was staggering. She was the caring mom for every kid who needed one, the mean mom for whenever someone's crazy needed to get shut down. I worked with her for six straight years and saw her get truly mad once. I've said so elsewhere and will say so again: she's the best teacher I've ever worked with.

Our Social Studies teacher Peter was a man of big ideas and no patience for adult bullshit. He saw our school and our classes in terms of their potential to be something better and worked constantly (when there wasn't a basketball game on) to shed all the stuff that didn't really matter. He was the first teacher I saw who centered social justice in his classroom in a way that promoted student voices above his own. He was nearly new when he started, and I almost instantly saw him as a mentor and leader. Still do. Always will.

Our Science teacher? Good lord. Ruth. I don't know why, but just about every one of the craziest people I know is a middle school science teacher, and Ruth is their queen. Students made dictionaries just to try to understand her. She was loud and ridiculous (her brain is apparently three overcaffeinated squirrels with their tails tied together). Also, she refused to let students do anything other than be amazing in her room. She taught science as an art, as a process, something you did, not just something you learned about. Ruth scared the shit out of me. Still does, but also she's probably the best worst person I know.

Our English teacher was me. In the classroom, I am some sort of cross between Fozzy Bear and that dude from the movie *Pi* (yes, the one who eventually gives himself a power-drill lobotomy just to calm his brain down).

Things were so very good because there is no right way to be a teacher except authentic. Wait. For real. There is no right way to teach, and we proved it every day by teaching four very different ways. There's no way for you to do it right except the way you do it.

Things were so very good because we could push each other and hold each other up, and because we had this beautiful thing where we laughed and worried and worked together. Things were good because we built strength upon strength upon strength, and the students who didn't like my sarcasm could get actual human care in math, or a science teacher who would walk them around arm in arm if they were late too many times, or a social studies teacher who welcomed, openly, every little bit of whoever they were. I wasn't having a good year with a great team: I was having a great year because of them.

Except, of course, then some stuff. Then there was this other teacher I was close friends with who I stopped being close friends with. (She, legitimately, was a jerk to me, but I did my best to keep it all quiet and not tell people about it, except the people I told about it.) But people notice, and people talk (because people are people and people are children).

Problem was, one of the people talking was talking a lot. This one teacher went all over the damn school to discuss his theories of all the awful things I had done or tried to do that had led to me and friend-teacher being me and former-friend-teacher. They weren't true, and I have no idea where he came up with them, but, you know, rumors are better than facts, and my name was suddenly in all sorts of people's mouths. Still, the problem was less what happened and more how I handled it. It bugged the shit out of me. Really, I was pissed for like a month straight while I focused on how wronged I felt and imagining that everyone was as obsessed with me as I am. My work suffered. My team kept me afloat, but it wasn't exactly a magically happy time to work with me.

Within a week of these conversations happening, my three major projects of the year were dismantled (two physically taken apart and put in closets). Later, I was offered an opportunity to transfer to another school, away from my team, and took it to transfer away from former-friend-teacher. Then, as happens, she got transferred to the same damn place, and I was without The Family, and things were suddenly much less good. So, you know, it was less than great, and I handled it less than perfectly, and it still stings when I think about it.

Plus, also, that same story told from the point of view of the no-longer-a-friend would likely sound completely different, and I'd be the asshole. But whatever. I wasn't.

***

WORK SUCKS SOMETIMES. There's no fix to make it all better except reminding myself it's just work. Some days I'm a better person, and I do things to support former-friend and still-boss because it's what's best for the school and what's best for the kids in the school. Some days I'm not a better person, and I want to do petty things just to watch people fail, and on those days I at least find the energy to stay very quiet and walk away.

Sometimes, surrounded by hundreds of students whose lives depend on you coming with your A game every damn day, you are tempted again and again to worry about the drama of the adults around you. Lately, I've just been reminding myself that I'd rather spend my time and energy on things that are constructive and creative rather than destructive.

No one is implicitly evil. There are not "right" and "wrong" groups of people, and you know what? We know that. We really know that, and we hardly ever act like it. I let the drama derail me from the best teaching team I can imagine, from three of the only grown-ups in the world I can stand, and I did it because I was acting like a baby. It would have been cool if I could have just been a grown-up about all of it. It would be cool if we just all acted like actual grown-up professionals at work. Instead, we make caricatures of the people around us. People are easier to understand when we reduce and exaggerate what we see of them.

In my building, for many years, there was tension between older and younger teachers. To the young teachers, brimming with energy, ideas, and overconfidence, the older teachers were often standing in the way of progress. There was some truth here. When new ideas were brought forward in staff meetings, that new idea was often picked apart ("We're already doing too many things." "We shouldn't do it if we can't do it perfectly." "Interesting, but in the past what we've done is . . ."). Our oldest (and loudest, and almost exclusively male) voices argued toward the status quo, and doing nothing new was often the only decision that made its way through the "So we'll think about that for a while." "Next year, maybe, if we start earlier . . ." "When things are taken off our plate first, then we can talk about . . ."

So to many newer teachers, the older teachers were cast as the cranky group. Their ideas and arguments, often borne out of real, actual wisdom, were dismissed as avoidance of ideas that were not their own. Of course, what younger teachers were missing was that many of the things that made the school successful, many of the best parts of our day or year, started as ideas from these older cranky teachers. Their arguments to do nothing were often arguments attempting to protect the programs they thought made our school special, ideas that only a few years ago were the new fancy ideas.

To the older teachers, the younger teachers were blinded by what they saw as an abundance of support especially for them. There was some truth in this. With a change in leadership in the school, the people being given the most input into building and district decisions were increasingly younger and younger (and almost exclusively female). Our building leadership team was mostly teachers with less than five years of experience (which, you can imagine, went over great with the veterans who literally built the place). Those younger teachers were often given the funding and support necessary to launch their new programs.

The older teachers, feeling suddenly ignored and diminished, dismissed newer staff as the "young, pretty things." There was some truth to this. There were some very attractive young teachers, but what the older group was missing about the younger group was that a large number of their ideas were very good. They were missing that a great idea ten or two years ago may not be the best idea today.

What most of us were missing was the fact that no one, really, belongs to a group wholly. What most of us were missing was the fact that no one enters education to do poorly, and no one goes to work just to ruin someone's day.

So here's what we did to make work less awful. A group of us spread across both groups but capable of non-jackassery made enchiladas and invited over a bunch of other people. We had a frank conversation about our school while drinking 200 percent more bottles of wine than was professional. We met each other around the table as people and not adversaries. It worked, for a time. We created a new leadership group, an official one, with representation from all over the building. We went to each other as needed over the next few years to smooth disagreements and come to understandings. We promoted good ideas and we worked to make them happen.

People enter education because they want to do amazing things for kids, but they never, or very hardly ever, do them all alone.

Crappy Job,
Great Career

LAST YEAR WAS A WEIRD YEAR among the staff of our high school. Our leaders, and leaders here meaning all four of us who had been teaching for longer than three years, were mired in a year of personal tragedy, financial crisis, and, in my case, acute self-involvement in the form of writing about all of my feelings all the time. This left a lot of younger teachers on their own to figure out how they felt about things. Many found inspiration in their work and each other, supported one another through stressful days, and pushed each other to be better. A few went another route and found all the different happy-hour deals within a three-mile radius. This group had a mantra, spoken all too often.

"It's just a job."

No wonder they were so salty all the time. I suppose teaching can be both a job and a career. I suppose during bus duty, or supervising a dance, or sitting through a meeting about setting up a meeting to discuss something sometime, I say to myself, "Fuck this job." But if the whole thing is a job, if the whole thing is *just* a job, you're doing it wrong. Teaching is a shitty job but a great career.

It's easy, so easy, to complain. I am in the years now when this was supposed to get easier, and just last week I almost cried twice. Nothing bad had even happened. I almost cried but didn't because I was just too tired. But it's worth it, ultimately, and actually way more than worth it.

There are the obvious reasons why. I get paid to have summer vacation. I'm sure different districts do things differently, but my paychecks are the same in July, when I'm pleasantly burning at a beach at noon on a Tuesday, as they are in February, when I fight through the snow for an hour for the chance to fight through an hour with kids who fought through the snow to be there. All bullshittery aside, I get paid pretty well.

I don't lift heavy things all day, or paint houses, or worry about how many widgets were made or sold or whatever. My job, the thing I'm paid to do, is to try to make kids better at things. There are people whose job it is to help me do that thing, and people whose job it is to make sure I'm doing my best to do that thing, but, mainly, for the most part I sit around and think of new creative ways for kids to think in new creative ways. I've painted houses before. It is better than painting houses.

People are good to teachers. There are discounts and appreciation days and all sorts of things like that. People give you a look when you say, "I'm a teacher," that they give nurses and cops, which is good company to be in (also, both those other jobs are way harder, I bet). I may be insanely naïve or lucky or sheltered or something, but the only time I hear about how bad teachers are is when teachers talk about how everyone talks bad about them. I don't see it. Then again, I'm a White man, and there is a different dynamic with the way people talk about and perceive women and people of color who are in the classroom.

Want a better reason to teach? A best one? Go ask three people who their favorite teacher in school was. Watch their eyes and listen to the way they talk about that teacher. You get to be that. Not for everyone, or even most kids, sure . . . but how many people do you need to touch in that way for it to be worth it? I have my number, and it is low. People come up to me sometimes, and they have run into a former student, or the parent of a former student, and I am brought up, and I am told wonderful things those students say about me, about my teaching, about what those students are doing now because of, in part, things they heard or did in my classroom. I've never once driven past a house I painted ten years ago just to see how it's doing.

Once I had a mom tell me that her daughter was alive at the end of a year because of me. A week later and unknowing of the previous conversation, the girl said the same thing. My being around at just the right time and not being an ass meant she was still alive. Just a job?

In fact, let's talk about her, because she saved me, too. I wasn't going to die or anything, but I was getting pretty damn close for the tenth time in my career to finding something else to do. I was in my first year in the high school after half a thousand years teaching middle school with the three best teachers I've ever met. I remember looking around staff meetings at the new school and thinking, "Yeah, I don't like any of these fuckers." They were good teachers, mind you, but I didn't like them, because I didn't like much of anything. Of course, those were adults, and I didn't get into teaching because I love sitting around in rooms of adults talking about teaching. There's always the kids, right?

In the second week of school, someone went into my desk and stole my phone. I gave an ill-planned, overly emotional speech to the class about the bond of trust we would need to form in order to blahblahblah. I was mocked. I was not a little mocked. I was severely, loudly mocked. I didn't get my phone back. But I did receive the delightful explanation that "no one cares about your shit." Indeed.

So it was that I was in my most defeated, my crankiest, my most fuck-this-job-iest when a student came to me and said, "Do you have a minute?" It should be noted that being all those things probably also meant enough of my own walls were down that I didn't look like the strutting blowhard I can often come across as. So I had a minute.

"I have to let you know, though," I'd seen the look in her face before, and this was not going to be a conversation about easy things, "I have a degree in English Lit, and a degree in English Education."

"So?"

"So I'm just saying, I know a decent amount about books

and writing and stuff, but I have no idea how to talk to people about anything other than books and stuff."

"Yeah, I have a therapist for that."

"Great, then I won't be your therapist. I'll be your English teacher."

"Fine."

"Do you want a granola bar? In addition to knowing a little bit about books and stuff, I also have granola bars."

That's how it started. She sat and talked to me for about thirty minutes. She told me about things that I won't share here, even in anonymity, because they're her things. I said a lot of things like, "That's awful," "No, it's not fair," and "No, I have no idea what that's like." Mainly, I just listened. I stared at my shoe and she stared out the window, and during every other prolonged silence, I offered her a granola bar. Later, I would figure out that it's helpful to throw down a big piece of paper and a bunch of crayons and sit and straight-up color with nearly-grown-people in the event they wanted to come talk about their feelings. I am really, really (I promise, really) crappy at problems that don't involve books. I'm not even that good at grammar stuff.

It turns out that she liked that I didn't try to fix it, and I didn't try to tell her everything was going to be okay, and I didn't treat her like it was my job to listen to her. She'd had poor experiences with all those things talking to the people whose job it really was to listen to her. So my room became a safe place for her to go when she needed to go somewhere, and often she didn't even talk to me while she was there. She would sit in a corner and draw, and I wouldn't give her grief about it, and I wouldn't try to sit and talk about feelings unless she wanted to, and then I mainly stared at my shoes some more. I introduced her to as many people in the building as I could who could be helpful, and they were. I stayed in touch with her parents, and we got through the thing as a team of people trying to get through the thing.

One time, she came up to me in the hallway and told me to hold my hand out. I held my hand out, and she dropped three shards of a razor into it.

"Did you use this?"

"No."

"Why did you give it to me?"

"I can't throw it away, but you should."

Just a job, though, right?

THIS GIRL, by the way, is going to change the world. She'll save more people than I will ever know. She'll be your hero someday. If ten bad life decisions and a couple of good ones led to me teaching in that school at the moment I needed to be there to help her by being a person, good. Screw everything else, it's totally worth it. It is beyond worth it. It is a privilege.

Last week I was sitting in front of school and a giant man yelled my name as he ran across the street. The giant man was Darnell, whom I met as a thirteen-year-old eight years ago. He ran up to me, lifted me up, broke nearly every bone in my body giving me a hug. I still have a letter Darnell wrote to me on the last day of school, thanking me for making him not hate English anymore and believing in him. I didn't tell him that, though. I just smiled like an idiot, and he smiled like an idiot, and then he had to catch a bus and was gone.

A parent came up to me at school once. She was there visiting her youngest, and her eldest was a few years removed from my class. He was heading into AP English this year. "AP! English!" She grabbed someone walking past, someone neither of us knew. "My son is starting AP English this year, and it's because he had this guy in eighth grade." She was crying just a little bit more than a little bit. She was all filled up with pride in her son.

A coworker came over one night. It was Saturday night, and she was thinking about teaching and I was thinking about teaching, so we thought about teaching together with some chips and hummus. She was in her first year and having trouble sleeping and having trouble relaxing or being productive at anything in the world other than teaching. She wanted to know when she would stop thinking about the kids all the time. "I dunno," I said. "Probably around the time that you should stop teaching." Cheesy. True.

My prep time for a few years lined up perfectly with sixth grade recess. There was this group of boys that met every day in the gym for recess to play basketball. One time, the rims were lowered in the gym enough that I could dunk on them, which I did. A lot. It felt amazing. You get to laugh as a teacher. You get to play and laugh a lot if you let yourself.

There's also this other one very not small thing: teaching makes you a better person. Really, the whole job is learning to understand and appreciate people, to say or do the thing that will move them from where they are to where they need to be, to build and manage and value relationships with humans, to care and believe in people, especially when they can do neither for themselves. You can't be the person other people need you to be without always making sure your shit is as together as it can be. Teaching requires that you work at being a person and work at understanding people and the world, and work at feelings and connecting and respect in ways and to a magnitude that is not often asked of adults who aren't bartenders.

In ten years, I've grown more as a person than as a teacher, but that personal growth has translated into my being much, much better at my job.

Also, every day that something god-awful happens in the world, I get to think about all the kids I know who are the ones who will make those things better.

There are lots of reasons why teaching is completely worth it. I can almost hear people say now, "Well, it sure ain't the money!" They will then laugh just a little too long at their perception of my poverty, and as their laughter trickles off, they will punctuate their point (for clarity): "Because teachers don't make shit." Yes, as a teacher, you will know people with nicer houses, cars, and more stuff than you. You can make good money teaching, but you won't get wealthy doing it. This should not surprise you. I mean, really, I don't imagine you could get as far as reading a book about teaching and think you could get private-jet wealthy by teaching.

Still, people joke too much, teachers joke too much, about the low-low pay of teaching. It's really not so bad. I will say something that almost no one will ever say (teacher or not): I make enough money. I mean, I work in a union school in a state that pays well and with a partner who has a job. There are very real situations where teachers are struggling to pay for essentials and needing extra jobs. My experience is that in my state and in my school, it's really not so bad.

Not only is the money not so bad, but joking too much about how little we make does distinctly bad things for teachers. We sound ungrateful for the money we make, and it is more than no money. There is a finite amount of the pie coming through public channels, and teachers make a good deal more than some, including some being paid to risk their lives. Also, except for a select group of suckers (administration, who work year round and deal with all the crummy parts of teaching [adults] without a lot of the best parts [kids learning new stuff]), teachers are the highest-paid people in the building. It's just a jerk move to sit and whine to support staff and custodians, none of whom is working less hard than you, about how double what they make is not nearly enough money for you.

When we joke about how little we make, especially around our students, we risk reinforcing that the profession we have chosen is a bad one. In the high school I went to, there was already an awkward divide between the new, shiny, show-offy cars of the student parking lots and the semi-old and very-old Hondas of the teacher lot. Jokes by the teachers made the money divide more obvious and more uncomfortable. (For others, I mean. My mom was a teacher's assistant then who drove a Geo, not even a kind of car anymore, and I got to school in a decade-old Toyota minivan that was shared among four siblings and is still in many respects the coolest car I've ever driven. I would trade the car I drive right now for one.)

So you don't make Lexus money when teaching, and most especially not while teaching and raising four kids by yourself. You do make enough money to have a car and a place to live pretty comfortably. That may not mean a lot to kids who come from wealth, who are people who teach out of a sense of service and stay because they respect the work and the profession (or quit when it's hard and stuff). But for someone who had less than everything growing up, my salary seems pretty great.

Recently, I've been trying to talk to my students about teaching in a way that speaks opposite the constant jokes about poor teachers. A recent conversation started because a class was asking/demanding a pizza party. I have never thrown any class ever a pizza party and was not of the mind to start. (I have allowed use of my lunch time and room to facilitate parties before, when the students figured out everything else and gave me a slice or two, but that's it.) These students in particular were asking for me to pay for everyone's food.

"There's no way I have the money right now to buy thirty kids pizza."

"Oh, right, you're a teacher."

True. I'm a teacher, and I am sometimes broke. I'm also an adult who made poor decisions about what house to buy and when, and I have a daughter who insists on eating and wearing clothes, and my wife and I have two cars that can have their keys locked inside of them in the same week, which requires two visits from the same locksmith, and sometimes it is two weeks before Christmas. So I'm broke for lots of different reasons other than my job. In fact, my job has been the thing keeping all those other things from falling apart/getting taken away for the past few years while my wife finished up her school and license to be a therapist.

I asked my students what they thought a good amount of money would be for an adult to make. They thought about it for a while, and I encourage you to do the same. I'll wait.

They came up with $50,000 a year. For many of my students, this is at least double their current family yearly income, and money that could buy them one heck of a lot more comfort than their lives currently hold. I like their number okay. Certainly, people could make more than that and not be upset at all that extra money they have to deal with. Certainly, people make less than that and lead fulfilling lives and still find the money to do the things most important to them, but $50k seems like enough money for a hard-working person to feel like they've earned what they make.

In my eighth year of teaching, I made just north of $58,000. I taught summer school again, which in my district is six weeks long, four hours a day, and will make enough to push me above $60,000 (it should be noted that Minnesota is a pretty good state to teach in). That is not no money. That's not crazy fantastic money, and it won't sustain a whole family at middle-class levels of stuff and weekly cell phone upgrades, but when I lock my keys in my car, I can call a locksmith, and I can pay the fifty bucks to have him open the door, and it's not going to ruin Christmas.

Also, during winter break, during which large chunks of this book were written, I will not work at all for sixteen days, and it will cost me no vacation time at all. I get another five days for Thanksgiving and another nine for spring break. I am counting weekends, because we never seem to, but I have often held jobs that assumed weekend work, and getting a job with two consecutive days off when the rest of the world was available to hang out was a pretty big deal for me.

Oh, yeah, plus summer.

Summer should maybe be its whole own chapter or, because of its power and importance, perhaps we should avert our eyes like it is the sun. That's how big summer is.

During the month of July, when I go almost nowhere that even rhymes with school (I don't like to swim), I am making the same amount as February, when only the Happy Light on my desk keeps me from losing my mind with stress and failure. February is why I need July, and I don't feel particularly guilty about getting the time off, but I do feel very thankful for it, and I do think it needs to be factored into the total package of the profession.

I work summer school because I kind of like it, and the extra money is good, and I teach in an enrichment program that lets me teach dorky classes about stuff I'd probably be sitting around talking about anyway (in my career, that has meant classes that focus on video games, *Star Wars,* and superheroes). I go to staff development and meetings about grading systems and new initiatives at school and welcoming new staff during the summer because I want to, and because I feel like all those things are part of the job, even if we don't get paid individually for each one. If I didn't want to do those things, I wouldn't have to and then would have nearly three straight months, nearly three full months, which is, unless I lost a month somewhere in there, nearly a fourth of the total year, when I don't have to work.

My mom taught while I was growing up, and every summer she would take her four kids, some tents, one of those big orange water jugs, and a half-ton of Kool-Aid to camp at a state park for three weeks. We became wild children who established whole systems of law, money, and justice built around bike tag (exactly what it sounds like) and a machine outside the general store that gave you a nickel for every soda can you put in. My dad didn't come because he mostly hated my mom, completely hated camping, and because there's no way in hell he could have taken that much time off work.

So I got these long trips with my mom every summer, and I'll get to take long ridiculous trips and work on projects that go nowhere with my daughter as she gets older. I don't know how much that is worth to everyone, but that's worth a lot to me.

Beyond the money, there's also the stability. This seems a fair point to admit that I have become old and lame enough to be really into things like job security. The kids are the first and largest reason, but the second biggest reason that I've never been seriously tempted to leave teaching is that I'm very, very sure I have a job next year and the year after that.

This is true because I have tenure, and depending on where and when you're reading this, what sort of licensure you do or don't have, or how successful I personally have been in pushing for reform of the tenure system, none of this may be true for you. In Minnesota, if you can keep from getting fired for three straight years while in the same district, you get tenure. Some districts do a whole lot of work with you in that time to see if you're doing great. I was seriously observed twice in three years and then got a letter saying that I was nearly impossible (for my small, monetarily strapped, administratively overworked district) to fire unless I really, sincerely, and repeatedly fucked up.

Yes, districts can and do fire teachers with tenure, but the process they have to go through is costly and gives the teacher many, many times to find their shit and figure it out. It is quicker and easier to fire a teacher if they punch a student, parent, or coworker in the face. Don't do those things. Short a physical assault, I figure it would take my district about two years and a ton of money to quit me if I just stopped teaching and started showing cartoons every day. In fact, if I just started showing cartoons every day, it may take my students and everyone else at least a week to figure out that I was doing anything different at all.

So I will likely not get fired. Losing my job, then, would come as a result of my district closing down (not out of the realm of possibility, as it is a funky district run by a few different school districts, any of which could pull out at some point). Were that to happen, I remain pretty confident that I could find another job doing what I do in another district, because we're going to need schools up and running until at least one year after the zombie apocalypse. With firing highly unlikely, and a school shutdown less unlikely but still a process that would take a while, I can sit and say with decent confidence that I will have a job for at least three years.

Few people, almost no one except teachers, get to say that sort of thing.

Few people also get to say that the measures of their success at work have nothing to do with money. At the end of the day of teaching, there is no tally of customers served, no long ticker tape being printed with the day's totals. At the end of the day, I think about the things that went well, and the things that were disastrous screwups, and I think about what to do better the next day. Every few weeks, I get money in my account, from work, but the money of the job and the job are divorced from each other in my head. I like and like and really like that.

Part II

FALL

There was a time in your life when you had friends,
enough time to read a book, and energy enough
to stay awake past 7:30 p.m. That time is not fall.
In fall, we uncover the work of the rest of the year,
we discover and ask questions we have little hope
of answering.

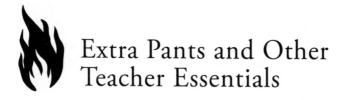

Extra Pants and Other Teacher Essentials

IN MY FIRST YEAR OF TEACHING, I kept a list of all the things I thought I would be good at other than teaching. I kept it on the desktop of my school-issued laptop and would look at it occasionally after a hard day or, sometimes, in the midst of a particularly rough hour. Though "juggler" was perhaps unreasonable and "Toby from *The West Wing*" was perhaps unrealistic, the list helped. Partially, I needed to remind myself that teaching was a choice I was making. I needed to remind myself that the frustration, that the one kid who just spent the entire hour staring at me as if she wanted to stab my face, that the early mornings and long days and weekends full of work and desperate attempts at sleep were things I *could* tolerate but didn't have to.

Sometimes I looked at the list because I wanted to start planning how to get out.

I'm convinced it's impossible to feel like you're doing a good job consistently through your first year. I've seen a few teachers who were convinced they were perfect right away, and they all got fired (because they were actually terrible), and no one was sad (except probably them). I don't feel like I'm doing a great job on lots of days. There are too many things going on for every one of them to go right. Failures are often exceptionally loud and dramatic, and successes are often delayed and measured in small bits of inches. Still, there are some things you can do to make it easier to be better right away.

THE TOOLKIT

I have a toolkit I buy at the beginning of every year, and I'm about to share it with you. Pay attention: this may be the only actually helpful advice I will ever give. Go buy these things (and here's why to buy these things):

Advil. (Obviously, but seriously: small inconveniences you used to power through may well now take that last bit of patience keeping you from losing your shit. In other words, even small headaches can make bad teachers.)

Mints. (This is particularly true if you are a coffee drinker. Don't be that teacher. Get some mints, use them. They are a work expense now.)

Tide pen. (Maybe for you, but it comes in handier for the kid focused on the new stain on their new shirt who you are asking to read someone's old poem.)

Lotion. (This took me a long time to figure out because I'm White. Lotion is nice when you're White, but when your skin is darker, dry skin is a big deal. I watched for years as Black kids would scour the school for lotion. Where would they find it? In the desks of the three or four employees of our school who were Black. Be a friend to Black kids, be an enemy to ashyness, buy a bunch of lotion, keep it out in your room for people to use. Do not be surprised when word spreads and students you do not have and do not know come to your classroom in the morning to use some.)

Pants. (You may already have these. If you have more than one pair, store one somewhere at school. An extra shirt may not be a bad idea either. By *pants,* I really mean any extra outfit. Why do you need these things at school? I don't know why you may need them, but if you ever do, you will be very glad to have them. My school used to do a monthly advisory period that mixed kids from many different grades together, and on one early fall day we played volleyball with giant beach balls and no points or rules but a ton of laughing from those of us who knew we weren't too cool for it. Unfortunately, my pants were not as eager as I was to try and spike the ball onto the head of a fourth grader. I'm pretty sure every person in the building heard the sound of my pants ripping. But I had extra pants, and the pants happened to be less than ten feet away. A quick trip to the locker room was better than spending the rest of the day on my desk chair wheeling around. Bring pants.)

DO NO HARM

For your first year, and probably your second, and probably every year after that, too, swear to yourself to do no harm. Be aware that you will break that oath, but do your best to fix it afterward.

When I was brand new to the profession, I taught eighth grade. The best thing about teaching middle school is that students are primarily waiting for their brains to start working again before they move to high school. This doesn't mean that there aren't great things to be taught, or that there won't be a thousand moments to do things that are memorable, life shaping, and inspiring that you can share with middle schoolers. Really, it means you have the freedom to do those things more often.

"But," you say, "the standards!"

Of course, but you probably shouldn't care about those that much.

"Whoa, but wait!" You are getting angry now. "My school says I have to care!"

Okay. Then pretend to care. Work around them. Do better things.

"You asshole!" you are screaming. "Have you read the math standards? No time! No time!"

I hear you. I do. You're screaming, remember? I hear you, but screw it. If you promise to try really hard to teach important things that matter to your kids instead, then screw standards.

Those of us in disciplines with standards that are based in skills and not content have it easy (English standards are more about how to read and write and not all the specific things you must read and write). I can do lots of different kinds of projects and still have the standards integrated. I mean, I'm pretty sure I'm doing that. In my first year of teaching I printed the standards out and had them displayed on the wall behind my desk, but I haven't read them since. Sorry (not sorry).

Standards, learning targets, and damn near all assessments come ultimately from a lack of trust in teachers. If they stop looking, of course, we would stop doing our jobs, of course. So a lot of the stuff we get saddled with at school ultimately comes from a place of fear from the people making the rules and laws, and they are often directed at teachers so bad at being a human they need to be forced to give a damn. There are some of those teachers out there, but not many.

I work near one rather amazing elementary teacher in her second year, and every day there's some website she's supposed to check to see what she's supposed to teach that day so her class can be just like all the other classes in the district. She doesn't think she should pay a lot of attention to that, because she'd rather do way cooler things. I very strongly agree. She could get lost in everything that she is told to do. She could get lost in hitting every standard every day, or she could make her room a rich place to learn. She chooses to, you know, teach. I bet she hits most of those standards, and I bet she has a ton of them, but I bet those standards aren't quite as crazy as secondary math standards. Those suck.

Math teachers, my message to you is this: you have two options. You can teach everything in the standards. To do this, you must go so fast through every concept that you mainly end up teaching a rehearsal of math and not real, deep knowledge of how math works. You will hit all the standards, though, in a way that each one of them will be spoken out loud in your room. Alternately, you can take your time with the most important concepts of the year, and you can make sure the kids really understand them and how to apply them and how they work and why they work. The better you get at teaching, the more things you can do, or at least you can get better at teaching the important things really well.

It seems to me that path one will serve only your ability to say in a meeting that will likely never happen that you hit every standard in your room. Your students will know fewer things because you taught them so many. The second path students will, I'm mostly sure, do better on tests and, this is the important point for me, will be able to do more math for the rest of their lives. Plus, it's what your kids need. If you aren't willing to get in a little trouble to do what's best for your kids, then really this may not be the book for you. I think you are less important than kids are.

You have to do no harm. Believe me, as a teacher, especially as a new teacher, putting a ton of pressure on yourself to achieve an unachievable goal that runs contrary to the way your students want to learn and the way you wish you could teach will not make you a happy person. It will not lend to great teaching. In that position, you run every chance of convincing students that they do not like your subject, or that they are just plain awful at it.

You've heard those stories before, right? "I thought I liked science, but then I had this horrible chemistry teacher and . . ." "I hated reading in school, but once I got out I realized . . ." Don't be that teacher. Your primary job is to show kids why your discipline is important and why people love it. You may not convince each and every student that Shakespeare is a fun weekend read, but they should understand why some people think so. They should know where their strengths are in your discipline, and they should be in a place as often as possible to show those strengths.

READ WITH KIDS

I've always had a standing rule with kids: I will read any book they hand me, provided they have read it too. This means I have read lots of really bad books about submarine battles. There is an unreasonable amount of submarine novels out there, and one of my middle school boys just couldn't get enough of them and couldn't find a sucker to talk about them with, until me. I read a whole fantasy series that had something to do with rings or a belt or something. A belt, I think. And gems? Something like that. I read that series for months.

Why?

Because it was worth my time, and so was going to performances, and playing kickball during gym and catching the second half of the basketball game after sitting in my room grading until dark. Teachers bristle sometimes about doing some of this stuff during their prep period, but this work is prep: it is some of the most essential work of teaching. Find dumb stuff to talk to kids about, then talk to kids about dumb stuff. If you see more than one kid carrying a specific book, make sure you read it. It will likely be awful, but read it anyway. This was the reason I read the *Twilight* series. I offer no excuse for reading it twice.

I had a student-teacher in my high school class who was really into comics and developed an amazing connection with a group of our kids by spending months trading comics back and forth. A thirty-second hallway conversation in which a student teases you for liking Daredevil even though he's lame and you tease her because she likes Deadpool who is way more lame can be the exact thing you need to feel like you belong where you are. Collect those little wins through the day, because you'll need them.

A TALE OF TWO TEACHERS

A few years into teaching, I was put in charge of two new teachers. Well, I was put in partial charge of those teachers. No one at that point would have trusted me enough to be in charge of anything by myself (that statement is just about as true today). I told each of those teachers the same piece of advice. I told them to do all the things they got into teaching to do. I told them to make big mistakes so long as they did the work to only make them once. I told them to give themselves time to figure out what they were doing, and in the meantime to do no harm.

That year was the tale of two very different teachers. Jenny became obsessed with her standards. There was homework for each day of the week and a quiz every Friday for Jenny to assess each student's learning. Students asked constantly, "Why do we have to do this?" and were answered more often than not with, "Because we're supposed to."

Let me start a new paragraph here just to highlight how awful an answer that is to a question. Students will ask constantly why they have to do an assignment or a class, or why they have to follow a rule or procedure. If your answer is "Because," you need to find a new answer or not do that thing.

Aside from teaching the students so many things that they learned almost none of it, and aside from overvaluing a very specific skill set in the process of grading, and aside from Jenny's classroom being so full of class that there was no time or room for any passion, Jenny created a spiral of work and stress that nearly drove her from the profession. Because of the sheer quantity of homework and quizzes assigned, she was grading during every available moment to try to keep up. Because the work was often uncreative and, to use an industry term, *worksheety,* grading was a soul-crushingly boring experience. Because Jenny was grading all the time, she felt like she was working all the time, and so she felt like she should be successful. When that work was not rewarded by creating engaged or high-performing students, she felt that she needed to work harder and harder until she had no more time or energy to give.

Jenny added a whole level of work beyond planning and

grading as well, the kind of work that is the truly exhausting part of the job. In the name of high standards, Jenny never ever let a single thing go. Every behavior blip became a behavior issue, and she stood rigid and unblinking in front of any explanation, any compromise. For some kids, those rigid expectations provide a safe and predictable place. For some kids, those sorts of expectations provide a predictable form of entertainment when they want a power struggle for any of the hundred reasons that kids do sometimes.

It's possible Jenny had never met a problem in life that was not solved by working harder, but teaching is just such a problem. Teaching is like trying to shove a couch that is too wide through a door. No amount of pushing harder is going to help until you figure out that you need to flip the damn thing on its side. Jenny spent the whole year pushing harder and harder on the couch, sometimes getting a good running start before slamming it against a doorframe it clearly would not fit through. She began charting her homework scores, creating intricate graphs and charts of student progress and homework completion. She started calling or e-mailing home whenever a student missed a daily assignment, and started staying at school until the janitors had to lock the doors. Still, the couch never fit. The doorway may well have been shrinking.

As an awful added bonus of awfulness, this teacher, this obsessively hard-working teacher, endured countless meetings with upset parents, countless comments from kids about class, and very little support from other teachers around her wrapped in a cocoon of their own problems. She did not eat lunch in the staff lounge, did not come out to events or happy hours with other teachers. Jenny worked. She worked and worked and things never got easier, and at the end of the year it cannot be said (believe me, I wish I could say) that she was successful. Students did poorly in her class, they remembered almost nothing of what they learned longer than a day or two, and, by and large, were not compelled at the end of their eighth grade year to sign up for honors or accelerated coursework in that discipline in high school. Jenny never learned how to flip the couch.

Teacher Two, Peter, was a very different story. Peter worked from the big ideas down. By that, I mean that instead of looking at eight pages of individual pieces of content and skills, he looked at the key three or four concepts he wanted to teach through the year. He thought about the things in his discipline that were the most important and the most engaging to students. He started his year getting to know his kids, getting to know what they wanted and needed, and gave them things that would push them to their strengths and then push them just slightly further.

Peter also had a ready-made instinct for picking his battles. When I have a student-teacher in my own room, I try to make them pause and ask themselves, before any conflict, "Is this the hill I'm going to die on today?" Sometimes it is. Sometimes you just need that hat off or that cell phone put away. Sometimes you just restate the expectation and then walk away without the demands for obedience, and you just go teach kids and stay calm and have a better day. The hill will be there tomorrow.

Peter also made full use of the community he was in, asked a thousand questions of successful teachers, and sometimes even of me. He reflected constantly on how things were going, how things could be done differently. He reshaped lessons constantly, tried different kinds of projects, different kinds of instruction. He flipped and flipped the couch, took steps back to see how the couch was fitting, and wondered if maybe the legs came off the bottom. There were times that he would leave to find a saw to maybe just saw the fucking couch in half. That's when we knew it was time to put the couch down for a while.

YOU WILL WANT TO GET DRUNK.
YOU WILL WANT TO GET FAT.

Two weeks into teaching, I was invited out for happy hour with the staff. I figured happy hour would be a laid-back affair and in fact remember having a conversation with someone on my team about whether or not it would be okay to order two drinks over the course of a couple of hours without seeming unprofessional.

We got to the place, which obviously ordered its cheese sauce, dartboards, and eagle statues from the same catalog. My professionalism worries were eliminated when most people ordered two drinks at once. *Jeopardy* reruns were on TV and people were downing shots.

A member of the support staff sat next to me. Her name was Linda, so I said, "Hi, Linda."

"Who the fuck is Linda?" She yelled at me. Yelled. Many people on our half of the table laughed.

"Sorry, I thought . . ." My face was attempting to crawl back in on itself, which made it difficult to talk.

"Linda is some bitch at school. I'm Terri!" It took me months, really, months, to work all that out in my head in a way that made sense. This was, in fact, Linda who was screaming at me that she wasn't named Linda. When she was out of school, particularly when she was out drinking out of school, she only answered to Terri. One time at school, I accidentally called her Terri and she looked at me like I was nuts, like she had no idea what I was talking about. Schools attract all sorts of exceedingly interesting people.

So here I was talking to Terri at my first happy hour. She stayed once I agreed that she was in fact, and obviously, not Linda, that bitch, and was, obviously, Terri. She talked to me for a long time, laughing very loudly at my jokes. Very loudly.

At one point, she laughed particularly loud and said, "Oh, I like this one." Which was nice, you know, to be liked. I had worried about that after not gelling particularly well with the staff in the school where I did my student-teaching. No invites to happy hours there, and no one saying (again, quite loudly) that they liked me.

The receptionist, who was sitting opposite us at the table leaned in and said, "He's married, Terri."

Terri looked me up and down one last time, said, "Aww, shit," and walked away. Actually got out of her chair and went to talk to someone else. The night kind of went from there.

***

EVERYONE DEVELOPS their own coping mechanisms. Linda had Terri, a complete escape from everything she did all day as a thoughtful, emotional educator who worked closely with a small group of elementary children who were pulled from their classrooms for extra math and reading. Linda was great, and I would grow to like her. Terri and I never got along.

I found it very difficult to avoid my own worst habits while teaching. Primary among those was the ingestion of nearly anything edible, all the time. In my first year, food was always everywhere. We had a common prep room with a few desks, a work island in the middle, and lots of drawers full of the half-finished projects of years past. One drawer was just for snacks, and we kept that drawer well stocked with candy. Most especially, there was always a fair amount of things with peanut butter covered with chocolate (the purchase of which, on reflection, was an overly large portion of my total earnings that year).

Our class periods were about sixty-five minutes long, and sixty-five minutes trying to focus twelve- and thirteen-year-old hormone bundles on reading, writing, or even just completing one full complete thought out loud was exhausting in a way that you feel in your teeth and shoelaces. I would walk from my room into the teacher office for a moment of air not tainted by angst, and there would be chocolate there. "Yes," I would think, "perhaps a piece of chocolate would be just the pick-me-up I need to face that exact same thing again, but you know, I've already had some today and it is only 9 a.m. I will wait," and by the time I had finished that thought I would have already shoved three pieces in my mouth and would be reaching for a fourth. On good days, I would sometimes eat enough candy to constitute an entire candy meal. On bad days, I would eat enough chocolate to kill a medium-sized shark.

During my first year, frantic nervous energy kept that chocolate from swelling me extremely, but over the course of a few years, it was hard not to notice that people were chuckling a little less when I made jokes about being chubby.

So the important thing is to recognize that unless you are the child of a firefighter who inexplicably always took you along to work, you are going to experience stress of a whole new kind in your first years of teaching. You may want to eat and drink a lot. I'm not saying you shouldn't do those things, but, you know, don't *over*do those things, and be aware that at some point in your career, if you plan on living past the age you'll be two years from now, you will need to find healthier ways to get by.

If you're already in your building, close your eyes, and imagine the staff who have been there for ten years or longer. Now focus on those staff members who still smile (without creating alternate identities for themselves). Go find out what they do to handle stress. They probably do yoga and drink tons of water and other stuff I find to be unreasonable requests of any human being. So, maybe find the ones who don't actively scowl at the sun and find out what they do instead.

Watch
Your Mouth

I'VE BEEN TEACHING LONG ENOUGH to watch the ebb and flow of slang words. Some, like a flash of lightning on a summer night, flood every small space in the world, command the attention of every living thing, hold their power for half of one breath, and are gone forever (like *YOLO*). Others, like herpes, arrive without fanfare, but once introduced, cannot be completely removed (like *petty*). There is one piece of slang with a particularly special place in my heart. The first time I heard it, I was giving what has become a yearly September speech.

The year before my first year of teaching, my dad died of cancer after a struggle that started in my senior year of high school. The anniversary of his death always falls in the second or third week of school, and though it has been almost nine years now, I can't seem to get through that day without some significantly deep quiet, a far shorter fuse, and at least three times the normal amount of awkward side hugs of the male teacher. To be fair to my students as best as I can, I give a little speech from the front of the room on or just before that day on why their delightfully grumpy teacher may be acting like an obnoxiously grumpy teacher.

"Oh, you're in your feelings." The voice came from the back of the room, more diagnosis than question.

"I'm what?"

"You're in your feelings."

One of my favorite things about slang words is that, among the people who use them, they seem so obvious so as never to be offered with an explanation or definition. In this case, none was needed. I was totally in my feelings. This phrase is used by students (as of this winter, mainly urban, Black students, which means White suburban students should be using it by summer or next fall) who are somehow emotional or vulnerable. Sometimes, it is a student who recently broke up with their significant other (or they were "talking" to someone and found out that person was "talking" to two other people at the same time, *talking* being a good example of a word offered without definition and whose precise definition in this context I hope I never, ever learn).

Sometimes, rather helpfully, a student will come to me before class and explain, "I'm just in my feelings right now," and I know to take it easy on them that day, maybe give them some space to work alone, or maybe offer an awkward side hug (I'm routinely told by students they are only awkward because I call them "awkward side hugs," which is just the way I want them). That conversation is a good example of why words are hugely important in interactions with kids. Both phrases, *in my feelings* and *awkward side hugs,* carry cultural importance in my room. Students understand that I am eager to understand the language of their friends, and so they will accept my own, often imagined, phrases in return.

Because language and culture are so strongly linked, as teachers, and specifically as teachers who serve students from different cultures from our own, we need to understand the importance of how we use, validate, and invalidate language in our room. This doesn't mean that we excuse students from using the academic language in academic papers they will need to use in college to write more academic papers (so they can eventually stop writing academic papers), but like most every other part of teaching, we can either wait (and wait, and wait, and fail and wait) for students to come to us, or we can meet them where they are.

As an English teacher and general nerd about words, I encourage a study of dialects in my room. By exploring the way people actually talk to each other, I can give students an understanding of the wide spectrum of dialects contained in a language. In many ways, english is less intimidating than English. When a teacher uses the phrase *proper English* with students, that teacher is calling all other dialects of english (which will often include the dialect of english that the student speaks at home and with the people they love) "improper." For students who may already struggle to feel a part of school culture, the assumption that their english is not the right english may just be one anti-invitation too many.

But when students are given a chance to study, present, and celebrate the words they say, you give them a tremendous opportunity to share their cultures. We spent three straight days once on the history and use of the word *finna,* a word that numerous White students swore they had never heard before even though it was said in front of them many times a day. We ended up referring back to *finna* (like, I'm finna go to the store, derived from the southern *fixin' to,* with roots in Creole and a whole bunch of other interesting stuff) all year long in just about every unit, as a cultural and racial marker, as evidence of the fact that culture is hard to see, and as something that was generally good for a laugh whenever I tried to use it in a sentence out loud (I'm so White I nearly sprain my ankle trying to say *finna*).

This doesn't mean you need to adopt the slang words of the students. In fact, don't do that. Please don't do that. There is space between judging and diminishing the language of your students and pretending like you're super down because you use it. That space is called the "not a dumbass" space. Live there. When you don't know a slang word, ask. When they answer, listen.

Talking about language in this way is actually a great way to share culture with kids. When you do, you will likely find that what different kids and families define as offensive or rude language can vary greatly. For example, when my mom called my name across the house ("Tom!"), I would answer "What?" When I answered that way, my mom would generally tell me what she wanted. But for some of my students, answering "What?" to a parent is roughly equal to saying, "I disrespect you greatly. You should end me." In my house, we could swear, but we couldn't tell each other to "shut up," which is probably why I talk so much.

Understanding the cultural roots of language is important to understanding what your kids are saying, or why they are reacting so strongly to something you just said. In a staff meeting the other day, I heard a teacher decry the "unnatural" language that students were using. I guess I should say that it was a White teacher who was talking about kids of color, but guess what? It kind of always is when shit like that gets said. Culture can be dangerous, in language, behavior, in expectations, because it's so ingrained that it feels natural. Learning to appreciate differences in language and how it can be perceived can help you talk to your kids better, and hopefully can help you avoid nearly getting fired like me.

In my second year of teaching, I was helping a small group working on a presentation. I wish I could remember what they were really working on. I wish I could remember what unit it was in, or even the time of year. I have no idea. I have no idea who any but two of the group members were, but I will never forget those two girls. The two girls were being jerks. I'm pretty sure they were being jerks. In the moment, at the time, I was 100 percent sure they were being awful people, but so many years later and tempered by their firm, angry belief that they were not being jerks, I question my own presumptions of the situation.

The girls were, I'm pretty sure, teasing another girl. The girl was talking about eating disorders, and the girls made a joke, I'm pretty sure they made a joke, about the girl having an eating disorder. I reacted poorly. I jumped immediately to anger, felt like I needed to shut this conversation down as soon as possible. I said, I know for sure that I said, "If you're going to act like idiots, you can get out of my room." It's the kind of thing that angry teachers would yell at kids all the time in the high school I went to.

So they left. They walked right to the principal's office. They had the principal call their parents and tell their parents that their teacher had just called them idiots. Which I didn't, but I kind of did, and, man, it was not long before the phone rang and I was being called out of my room. A sub was on the way, I was told, for as long as it took.

Over the next couple of days, we had a few meetings, the principal and I. Our final meeting included the students and the mothers of the two students. I explained that I was sure, pretty sure at least, they had made a joke about eating disorders. I explained and explained that I did not call the girls idiots but simply presented them a choice that if they were going to act like idiots, I wanted them to leave. "So you called my daughter an idiot." "No, like I just said, I told her IF she was acting like an idiot . . ." "So you called my daughter an idiot." "But see, they were making fun of this other girl . . ."

They were all very kind, really, dealing with just how dim-witted I was being.

No one in the room, myself included, thought there was truly a large difference between calling someone an idiot and suggesting that someone may be acting like an idiot. Either way, the word *idiot* had been thrown at a kid. It took me too many meetings to understand, admit, and repeat three times, "It is never okay for a teacher to even suggest that a student is an idiot." It was the strongest truth in the room, and without putting it on the table, nothing else could be resolved.

The moms, both Black women, explained to me (and then explained again slowly and using small words when I didn't get it the first time—because, let's be honest, only one person in the room was acting like an idiot, and it was the only teacher there) that as Black women, the level of their intelligence was assaulted constantly in school, in media, and in society. Calling, suggesting, or even pointing in the direction of anything like the word *idiot* directly reinforced a very real expectation they too often saw from teachers. Calling their daughters *idiots* was not just mean, was not just stupid: it was powerfully racist.

Holy shit, guys. When you make kids mad, or when you

make their parents mad enough to drive over to school and talk to you, listen. Listen, listen, listen. Other teachers will circle you, most likely, and tell you all the reasons you are right and the parents are wrong, because it sucks to have people be mad at you, and teachers are used to working hard to make bad feelings go away. Comfort is not a bad thing, but do not let yourself be comforted away from serious reflection. Listen and listen, because there are words that you may use that have a power you do not understand.

They were right, of course, and though I did not deserve their attention or their time or patience in teaching me, I was grateful for it. I grew slowly to understand that words had such larger power behind them because they played into a history of negative expectations. Sure, the easiest answer is to maybe, just for fun, not call any of your kids names. That makes sense. Still, name-calling or not, language and culture are tied together, and it's important to stay aware of how you may or may not be excluding or showing preference for a culture in your room.

Last year, for example, the teacher next door was a fan of playing devil's advocate in a way that let him push his worldview on kids rather aggressively. I've seen that work well, saying the thing that will rile the kids up, get them talking. I've seen it work well, but really only like 5 percent of the time. Generally speaking, being the devil's advocate means saying, "I'm not a complete asshole, but if I were, I would say this." It doesn't play well with students, or anyone.

One day, when a discussion of World War II went (predictably) to Caitlyn Jenner (I mean, every time, right?), the teacher next door decided to play devil's advocate. It started with a student saying that Jenner was being too public, that "that gay stuff" was being pushed in the student's face too often even though they "didn't believe in it."

These moments happen in school. Students will say things that many will find offensive. You feel the class tighten. The awkward pause you take trying to figure out what the hell you're going to say as a response will feel fifteen minutes long. Early in my teaching, I would have pulled the plug on the whole thing, yelling over students if necessary to say, "Nope nope nope, we're not talking about that."

As I got more comfortable with the rather challenging notion that students are whole human beings who live in the same real world I live in, and that school could be used as a place where those human students could bounce ideas and perspectives off each other, I started to try to let those conversations happen in my room. It's not always super clean and painless, but it can sometimes be really important.

The most important thing you can do in those situations is do your best to take care of all the students in the room. Sometimes, those students will be very loud and obvious about the help they need, but more often it is the students sitting quietly, sinking into their seats, who need you thinking about them. Students who may not want to put themselves in a position to have harmful things directed at them, who may not want to enter into a classroom discussion about what makes them different, who may not want to out themselves for the purposes of a spirited debate.

To the students who "didn't believe" in "gay stuff," I might ask what they think it would feel like to be a gay student in the class who heard that comment. I might even explain some of the history of trans rights and trans violence as a context for why it may be important to many people that Caitlyn Jenner was so widely and loudly accepted. I'd be careful to steer the conversation away from "right" and "wrong" and toward an understanding of mutual perspectives. It has been my experience, at least usually, that students who have voiced problematic statements about race, class, gender, sexuality, or bodies seem to do so reflexively, but when brought into a non-blaming conversation that investigates more deeply, they tend to reveal that they are far more understanding than their first comment suggested.

Really, though, it's not about that student, the student who said the thing. It's more about those quiet kids, waiting and watching to see if the statement that offended them will be challenged in any way, waiting to see if your room is a place they can be safely themselves. There's a difference between engaging in an open conversation with students like that, and feeling the energy that offensive comments can generate and thinking, "Yeah, let's amp that up a little."

That's the only thing I can imagine he was thinking when the teacher in that social studies classroom responded to the student by saying, "And think about his wife. Does anyone think it's rude to live a lie like that for so long? Think about those people whose husband is actually gay, or whatever, and their whole life is turned upside down when he decides to tell the truth."

This was a thing that got actually said in an actual classroom. I did not hear it, but I heard the response to it. From my room. With both doors closed. There are so many things in there that we'd really need a white board and a long weekend to pull it apart, from the continuing to refer to Jenner as "he" to the idea that people are somehow maliciously keeping their sexuality a secret while building up a life with another person just so that one day they can play a big joke on straight people by screwing with their life. Of course, those sorts of transitions have always played out entirely positive for the person coming out, right? So, just like that, one comment can be the sort of violent thing a student will remember for the rest of their lives.

Oof.

What followed was less a group of students loudly disagreeing with the teacher and more a small group of emboldened students bashing homosexual and transgender people until the bell rang. When it did, a group of four students entered my room looking like they had been kicked in the stomach. Looking, really and not metaphorically, like they were going to throw up and also punch all the faces they could find. This was the quiet group, the group that sat in the corner and listened to their classmates debate their right to full humanity with the casualness of a Coke-or-Pepsi debate and with the endorsement of the teacher to do so. In that quiet group were students who were transitioning or had transitioned, were students who were gender queer and thought and fought hard against the idea that gender must be a binary and static thing.

In that quiet group of students was a tremendous amount of badasses who were feeling horribly unsafe. It wasn't just that class and not just that conversation. These are students for whom going to the bathroom is an unnecessarily and shamefully difficult experience (shame on us, not on them). These are students whose schools can't or won't change their names on rosters to their preferred name, so every hour with a sub will be a slap across the face during attendance (unless their teacher thinks ahead half a second and leaves behind edited rosters or something, pretty please). These are students who are yelled at by staff for holding hands while walking past cisgender straight couples with tongues in each other's lungs. These are students whose humanity is not and should never be a subject of debate. So much of the way that we inflict harm on them is in the words we use and the ways we use them.

My class that day turned into a healing circle for students, most of whom were in social studies the hour before, all of whom had heard what had happened. Students expressed anger and worry and vulnerability and support and apology. We healed because we weren't going to learn until we did, and because as a teacher I feel responsible for my coworkers and protective of my students. The kids decided they didn't want to talk to that teacher, and they asked if I would instead.

When I took their concerns to that teacher later on, he was upset that they hadn't spoken up in class. Really, that was pretty much his whole response, over and over again, "Why didn't they say something? It could have been a really great discussion." I don't usually like to bring up the mistakes of other teachers (usually because I have plenty of my own to pull from, and because I don't like to sit back and smack-talk others), but fuck that guy.

A helpful hint to teachers: if you suggest or openly declare that a student isn't the right kind of person, they probably won't treat the discussion as a fun intellectual puzzle.

We're big enough kids, or should be, to understand that the intent of what we say can differ greatly from the impact of those words. As a new teacher, I struggled mightily with sarcasm (this may be easy for you to imagine if you've read this far). Kids were downright scared of me, because they had no idea if I ever meant what I said. I had the option to just do what I do and let kids figure it out, of course, because I don't think anyone's ever been fired because of sarcasm (though I could have been the first). But here's the thing, *the* thing: our rooms are not ours. Our rooms and our schools belong to our students.

It is, I suppose, our right to do exactly what we feel like doing as an adult in the room and blame the kids when they can't adjust to our sarcasm, or our tough love, or whatever our thing is. It's our right, the system supports it, but it's a shitty way to teach, and we know it. It is our job to adjust the way we talk, teach, and act to be exactly what each one of our students needs at any given time. It is an impossible and incredibly frustrating job, but I swear to you, it's the only way to do it right.

We will, all of us, make mistakes, all of the time. Just this week I was talking to a Native student and remarked that I loved the way she talked. It reminded me, I said in my super-White-guy way, of the way people spoke in the movie *Smoke Signals,* almost musically.

"Awwwww," her friend chimed in next to her, "he said you talk Rezzie."

Rezzie like reservation, like the way people talk on reservations, like not in a way that this student thought was a nice thing for me to say about her friend. I had no idea that was a thing. That took some listening and some question asking and also just a lot of me feeling like a jackass and wondering why I would ever think it was a great idea to talk about someone's speech or accent or slang or sounds without really knowing a damn thing about them.

We can't be so afraid of making mistakes that we don't speak at all, but we also, at all times, need to watch our damn dumb mouths.

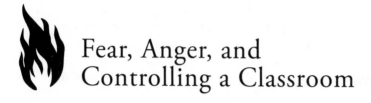

Fear, Anger, and Controlling a Classroom

I HAVE A PRETTY GOOD FRIEND ON STAFF. He is a newer teacher—talented, committed. He calls himself a citizen of the world (I've never heard him do so out loud, but he wears soccer jerseys an awful lot, so I'm extrapolating). He's developing new, big ideas for his classes; he's teaching social justice and social agency. Everything would be nearly perfect, says the thought bubble from his white knuckles, if only the kids would let him teach.

"It's like they're not even scared of us," he laments after class, and though he and they deserve more from me at that moment, I keep my thoughts on fear silent. I play the part of the good coworker and do my best to sympathize and support, give the teaching advice equivalent of "Drink more water," and walk away before saying, finally, and too quietly, "They shouldn't be scared of us. They shouldn't be scared of us," as if saying it twice will make him hear it.

On one far side of a spectrum is "They're scared of me," and on the other is "They like me." In the meaty middle, not touching either of those statements, is "They respect me." Though liking and fear are often confused for actual respect, neither is particularly helpful in the classroom. I've gone for both, and neither has worked very well for anyone involved.

It's easy to understand why we want kids to be scared of us.

Fear is about control, and as teachers, especially as young teachers, it feels as if the very most important thing we need to do is control our classroom. For me, and I would guess for many, teaching was the first real position of authority I was put in, and I wore my authority with all the puffed-chestiness and entitlement I felt should be afforded a teacher. I was, after all, an adult, at the front of the classroom no less, and I was wearing khakis. What else could one possibly need to show or do to establish authority?

Some of that assumption of respect, or maybe most if it, even, had to do with my Whiteness (which was also responsible for the khakis). As a White kid who went to mostly White schools with mostly White teachers and always White administrators, I afforded respect to those in authority because I had been taught through experience that nearly anyone in authority anywhere I may place my precious White butt was there to help me get whatever I wanted.

So when I assumed my own room and assumed my own name tag, I assumed everyone would listen just because I had some very important things to say (or at least because a very important person [khakis] was saying them). When things didn't go the way I expected, I got scared and, in my fear, got loud and angry. Because I insisted on establishing and holding my allotment of power as a classroom teacher, I was a walking invitation to any student looking for a power struggle.

The problem with power struggles is that only in the best schools with the best administrators is it possible for students to win. As a teacher, because we know we usually get to win, because I knew I usually got to win, most of my arguments (even or especially the ones I thought were particularly well argued or effective) came down to some form of "Because I said so." This was especially true and especially infuriating when the student was completely right. I remember a student in my first year, Max, who said (I remember because of his politeness), "Excuse me for saying, but this seems like a waste of time." We were about three weeks into a creative writing project that would last another two weeks and should have been capped at, maximum, three days. His statement was well aimed to perfectly and unintentionally hit at the core of my insecurity.

The writing project, which sought to pool small selections from each student in four different classes into one coherent novel, involved very little writing and very many skills that would only be helpful the next time they wanted to write a novel with a hundred people. It was a wreck. I knew it, they knew it. The math teacher next door knew it would be awful well before I started but didn't warn me because she thought I should learn by making mistakes and because she didn't think I would heed her warning since I thought my idea was so damn good. She was right on both counts, and I don't think I'll ever forgive her. I have her eldest son in my class now, and reliving this unit has convinced me to say something cruel to him tomorrow.

Anyway, everyone involved saw it was a disaster, but Max was the first student to say so to my face, so frightening was the sheer weight of my enthusiasm. Oh man, did I let Max have it. I used guilt ("I'd think at this point of the year and after all I've done for you, you would trust me to do this"). I threatened with grades. I acted disappointed and angry, and I was, really, just a complete dick about the whole thing ("I know this isn't worksheets and memorization: this is real creativity" [it wasn't], "and you may be resisting because you struggle with that"). Seriously, I did all those things, and all at once, and all of them were my saying, essentially, "Because I said so."

Sorry, Max. You were right to speak up. You deserved a better answer, and I would give a better one now, I promise. Also, that unit was pointless. Total waste of time. My bad.

My reaction was so excessive because the question threatened so greatly an illusion I tried so hard to pull off. I really and sincerely thought I had not yet been spotted as a fraud. I pretended I knew what I was doing up there. Everything was according to plan. Everything, absolutely everything, was completely under my control. Any assault on that illusion was met with a shock-and-awe level counterattack. I wanted the kids to try because they wanted to, but if they didn't want to, I was fine with their trying because they were scared not to.

Another day, some students were working near my desk and found my phone. They took a goofy picture of themselves and set it as my phone's background. Holy shit, I went ballistic. Scared of god-knows-what beyond kids reading texts about how I fell asleep before 9 p.m. every night that weekend, I screamed, downright and outright screamed at a class of mostly twelve-year-olds about invasion of privacy. I screamed about the suspensions one could receive and deserve for such a thing (untrue), about lawsuits (lawsuits, I say!) against anyone going through any of my things, physical or digital. Yes, I threatened to sue kids, and then threatened again in the next class hour, just to be sure. I was tightly wound in those days, and my god did it feel comforting and powerful when kids acted scared of me. And when I screamed, they acted scared of me, but they didn't learn better, and they surely didn't respect me.

It gets worse than that, of course, and because I've blocked all such instances of my own assholery from my mind, I'm stuck telling the story of another teacher from just this summer. This year there was a fire drill. In summer school, the student body is maybe a fourth the size or less than it would be during the school year. The smaller group of students is divided into classes half or less the size of a school-year class. Fire drills, never exactly the providence of chaos one might think, are remarkably, exceptionally relaxed things during our summer program. There are far fewer kids to be potentially engulfed in flame and, since a lot of the kids aren't from our district, far fewer kids whose safety even matters (jokes!).

My class made our escape through the back doors and was joined shortly by another smaller group. This group was younger kids, maybe seven to nine years old, and was taught by a perennial pain in my ass. The guy doesn't teach at my school but thinks the summer school deal is a good gig. (I should mention I'm teaching a class on superheroes and getting paid for it.) Thing is, he is a shit teacher. I taught next to him three summers in a row, and he was such a shit teacher that my room started to stink.

This dude is a yeller's yeller, carrying and threatening with a metaphorical stick that would go up his ass if he could only relax long enough to get it there. I'm generally a nice person (not really), but there's a special spot of fiery anger I keep reserved for teachers who make kids feel bad. So this guy earned that anger during this fire drill. His class grouped around him in a tight circle, all of them except one young, awkwardly haircut boy who made the mistake of being the outlier.

"I said, 'Follow me.' Did you hear me say to follow me? So why didn't you follow me? No, you didn't. No. You. Did. Not. Why did you end up way over there if you were following me? Do you understand what *following* means?"

The guy was yelling. The kid is probably seven.

On the way back in the school, he made the kid follow him in, literally made him walk a foot behind him like a duckling while the teacher wound his way in circles around each table in the cafeteria and the rest of the class stood and watched. This happened in real life, in my real life.

It's hard to fully quantify just how shitty I felt at this moment, and now, writing this down. I've done a poor job here of showing the derision in that teacher's voice, in the complete demolishing he laid on this little kid, and a poor job of showing just how little I did about it. Back in my classroom, I talked to my kids (they witnessed the whole thing) and told them that it was never okay for a teacher to humiliate them, to yell at them. But shit, I told that to my class to make me feel better, not them, and it didn't really work. Why?

Because shitty things feel shitty, that's why. The truly sinister aspect of this sort of teaching, this heavy-handed bully bullshit enforcement of White cultural authority masquerading as "high expectations," is that more likely than not the rest of the class blamed the kid and not the teacher. Didn't he know to pay attention, to be quiet, to get work in on time, to talk without attitude, obey without pause or question? They blamed the kid and were mad because he made class just that much more uncomfortable for them, and the kid (who is often the kid with low skills, or who struggles with traditional class structure, or is from a different culture or is a different color from the other kids in the room) gets punished again at recess, in the lunch room, or on the bus.

Oh, and those quiet kids' parents? They love that teacher. When you walk past his room, the kids are quiet, the kids are respectful, obedient; the kids are what every person who knows nothing thinks they should be: busy. The kids are also terrified, and years from now they will remember little else from the year than how scared they often were.

I stopped talking about summer school a while ago there, you may have noticed. I'm talking about me on my worst days, and too often during too much of my worst years. My students often call me "Mr. Rad," but during the year that my very small daughter decided sleep wasn't her thing (and so, not my thing) they started calling me, with very good reason, "Mr. Mad."

Oh, kids. Dicks.

I'm talking about a composite of former teachers and current coworkers who ascribe to the philosophy of fear to rule their classroom. May they all, and me included during those years, go to hell. There is no amount of quiet worth doing harm to your students.

THERE ARE A FEW THINGS I've learned along the way to calm myself when I've needed calming. I imagine these sorts of fixes are different for everyone, but I've felt a steady decline in the amount of anger I've felt at school, and the level of frustration I've felt while dealing with difficult situations (especially with students).

My growth from the Hulk into Bruce Banner started with a mantra. I am not a *mantra* person, really, and I may well be using the word incorrectly here. When I feel myself getting ridiculous, when I feel my voice rising or my tone getting that extra kick of aggression, derision, or annoyance, I say to myself (and sometimes right to the person I'm talking to), "Anger is not righteous." I'm not big on the word *righteous* as a general rule, either, but I've found the word connected with the main reason I got mad so easy: it felt good and powerful to be mad, and being mad often made the things I wanted to happen happen faster. What I needed to remind myself was that there is always a better way, a practice that better matched my philosophy, a conversation that wouldn't be damaging to anyone.

That's a surface-level fix, and one that was easy to do at the beginning. As I really took the mantra and started to experience weeks and months in my classroom without a raised voice or angry comment, I found myself missing the confrontation less and less. In fact, as is true with most arguments, the further I got from the confrontation, the sillier it looked. This perspective helped me avoid anger wasted on little things, which helped build positive relationships with students instead of those based on fear.

I swear to you that this is true: the fewer times your students hear you yell, the more likely they will be to want to hear you talk.

So I yelled less and got angry less and worried less about the little things ("I said I wanted you/that/those here/there/away," "You said this/that while I was doing something other/different," "You need to have more/less/none of that shirt/shorts/hat"). I also somehow found a small amount of humility about my teaching, was able to let go of the ridiculously silly illusion that I had everything under control. Because of that, I learned a very important and very powerful thing: I learned to admit I was wrong, and to say I was sorry. I'm from the Midwest, where we say sorry for asking for water at restaurants, for contracting illnesses, but not for hating someone, cheating on someone, or, it turns out, for screaming at someone.

This year, my school went through renovations of the area I worked in, renovations in the "looks like a nice hotel" range. We were very protective of our pretty new space, and there was no confusion that teachers were to be held personally (and spiritually) responsible for any stains the new space might develop in the course of housing hundreds of teenage bright ideas. So it was that I reacted strongly to a student bringing (gasp!) and opening (gasp! gasp!) an energy drink (ick, but whatever!) in my class.

If I remember correctly (again, my instinct is to desperately and immediately forget when I screw up), I walked up to him, snatched the drink from his hand, and told him I'd be throwing it out as soon as I could find a trash can (it's the little things that get missed in renovations). His response was stronger than my response and involved some very gracious (if strongly delivered) invitations to a power battle along the lines of "No, you fucking won't."

So, you know, things were going great.

We went back and forth in front of the class for two or three comments before day one of teacher school training kicked itself into gear, and I thought that, just maybe kinda, it was a bad idea to be doing this in front of an entire classroom. I told the student to wait for me outside, and he offered another gracious, tempting invitation: "I'll just go to the office." But, no, I hate sending kids to the office. In that moment, I had trouble remembering why I hate sending kids to the office. Doing so would have meant the end of a conflict, a quieter classroom, and an angry student who was someone else's problem. Then I remembered, for all those reasons, and for the fact that it sets up a really screwy power-discipline dynamic that I don't like, I don't send kids to the office unless violence is involved or threatened.

He stood in the hallway for the minute it took me to get the class directed on whatever we were working on next, and holy shit, you should've seen that kid's face by the time I got out there.

Had I been seeing straight, I would've seen a hundred interactions like this written on this kid's face. I would have seen a history as a Black boy in schools full of teachers who didn't trust and respect him in the automatic way they do the White girls. He was equal parts entirely unsurprised and furious and humiliated, and, had I been seeing straight, I would have recognized that. But in that moment, and with that kid, and on that day, I made it all about me instead. Our conversation started with all the things he did wrong. Actually, it wasn't a conversation. Of course it wasn't a conversation. My half-yelling at a kid who wanted to punch me or cry or both started with my telling him all the ways that he was wrong. At some point, I'm pretty sure I pointed to a couch and said that it was worth three thousand dollars, and pointed to myself and said, "It's my job to make sure that couch is this nice next year and five years from now." Right, because *that's* my job.

I said the phrase, "We have a school to run here." Jesus.

Thank god I said that bullshit phrase. The bullshittyness of that phrase snapped me out of the tirade I was on, reminded me that it was not in fact my job to protect furniture or to run the school, and most especially, it was not my job to make this kid feel awful for any reason. So I stopped. I took a breath.

I apologized. You should've seen this kid's face then, too. I apologized for yelling, for attacking, and I apologized for not giving myself a chance to listen. I asked what was getting him so upset, what got him so upset in the classroom. It took a few minutes to bring him along on my sudden change of direction. The sheer tonnage of emotional momentum of a teenager is difficult to maneuver quickly, but we got there. I made him sure that I wanted to really hear what he had to say, made him sure that I wasn't looking for another angle to yell at him for.

He told me I embarrassed him. Of course I did, and of course I didn't realize it. Of course it was embarrassing to sit in class and have a teacher come and take a drink away from you, rub in the fact that there was nothing he could do about it, make a fantastic display of who was powerful and who was not. What is more stupid-teachery than passing judgment or punishment on someone without giving them a chance to talk? Of course I didn't realize it. This was my first year in high school, and it didn't occur to me that the tough-looking Black boy could be humiliated by some little thing (because of my own shitty anti-Blackness, really, an idea deep in my head, backed up by a bunch of research that White people consider Black people less able to feel pain). All these things fed that moment, and it's hard as hell to admit it, and recognizing it doesn't make it a single bit better or more excusable.

It didn't occur to me that thousands and thousands of these little humiliations were what made this teenage boy try to look and act tough. I knew these things, but knowing them at a workshop and using them in the hallway when someone told you to fuck off are two different things.

Teaching well is a whole lot of thinking, and then thinking, and then getting it wrong, and then reflecting, and then trying again. As a general rule, I make fewer mistakes when I remember that kids are people.

He talked about how he felt in the classroom when I took his drink away, when I talked to him like he was an awful kid for having a drink. I listened. I apologized for specific steps along the way so he knew I was serious (because "I'm sorry you're upset" never cuts it). I talked about a lot of good things I had seen from him that week that went by without comment the first time. He listened. He came back from the brink, and so did I. We left it somewhere around the neighborhood of, "Huh, that wasn't the best. Let's not do that again."

From that point forward, he went from a D to an A student, and I never had a single problem with him again. In fact, he went on to be president of three colleges at once and discovered a hidden city of unicorns during a hospital-building charity trip to a continent he discovered.

No. Not really. But most books and professional developments and stories from people who have left teaching follow a pretty similar and ridiculous structure: (1) student is failing or struggling in some giant way and usually their parent has, like, been eaten by wolves or something on the kid's birthday; (2) teacher says the exact right thing to the student; (3) student is all the way better forever and ever; (4) teacher never makes a mistake again.

So, actually, we had some problems here and there during the rest of the year, but nothing we couldn't handle. He knew I respected him. I really respected him. I got respect back, and when I really needed to, I could get him to try harder on a paper or help another kid out. He was a 5 to 10 percent better student for me. I was a 5 to 10 percent better teacher for him. Better is better than worse.

The path to a "managed" classroom will be harder if you try

to meet every student where they are and understand what they need, but the path is worth it.

I WAS OUT FOR HAPPY HOUR recently with a group of teachers, many in their first year or new to the school. I had fried things and dark beer in front of me so was doing a poor job of engaging in the conversation, instead focusing on the glory that is cheese wrapped in bread that is fatty and crunchy.

The teachers were reflecting on their weeks. There was a student who had a blowup in class; there was a class that was one big train wreck. One teacher mentioned that for the first time ever, he yelled at a class. He yelled loud enough, he said, that he scared the students silent.

To his credit, he felt bad about yelling and addressed it with the students the next day. Of course he yelled, and of course we all do, because teaching is like putting together a puzzle without all the pieces on a table that is too small. Also, the puzzle is on fire. So of course we get tired and frustrated and sometimes it just seems like too damn much to give students patience when you already spend nearly every waking hour of your life trying to figure out how to make their lives better. Of course we yell, but we shouldn't. We should not. It's one thing to make mistakes and another thing to embrace them.

The other teachers around the table really perked up at the mention of a class that quiet. The first teacher said he felt bad about yelling and was instantly given a free pass from everyone. "Sometimes they just need that," was the prevailing sentiment at the table. The other teachers talked about their biggest blowups or wished that they could sound meaner when they wanted to.

Somewhere in the middle of the conversation I cut in. I was that teacher for a few minutes. I was that teacher trying to offer helpful advice but coming off as demeaning. I was that teacher who won't let people blow off steam at happy hour and comes around with that same earnest, "It's all about the kids" shit that teachers always say. I'm often that teacher, I am, because their feelings are more important than ours. I got to be that teacher who said, "It makes sense when you feel like things are going wrong to resort to fear and anger, but the problem isn't that you yell at a kid now: the problem is that in ten years you're going to be really really good at it."

I've had that teacher, you've had that teacher. The teacher who got good at scaring, intimidating, and humiliating students, so much so that they very rarely need to do it with a raised voice. That teacher may have classes that look successful, but everyone around them knows that the students are just scared.

Of course, we've all had the opposite teacher as well, the teacher who found early on that making kids like you is the easiest way to have a pleasant (though rarely productive) day. I sought this sort of approval in my first few years at least as regularly and as energetically as I did fear and unquestioned obedience. I must have been a very confusing teacher.

Just like the angry teacher, the teacher who wants to be friends with everyone can fool themselves into feeling productive without really helping anyone. Teaching involves conflict. Real learning happens when someone is pushed out of their comfort zone, when someone takes a leap at something they didn't think they could do and are not allowed to fail. People do not often go to those places willingly, and so teaching often feels like conflict. When you get good at being the cool teacher, you get good at avoiding any instance that may result in something that feels like conflict. You steer your class and your interactions to a comfortable place where everyone does whatever they're used to doing. It makes for more laughing, less stress, friendlier interactions, and not a lot of learning.

If I have a failing as a teacher (and who am I kidding with the *if,* because of course I have many failings as a teacher), it is that I lean too heavily toward the attempt to be likable. It's easy, because many students will constantly reaffirm behavior that allows them to get away with doing less than they really should.

Earlier in my career, I often asked a goofy question of the day while I took attendance. It was a nice way to get to know kids, but I eventually got rid of it because kids got wise to just how easy it was to parlay the questions into side conversations that I would indulge for most of an hour (oh lord, the number of class hours I have wasted completely and chalked up to "community building" when I damn well knew better). One of my favorite questions early in the year is which superpower each student would want if they could pick one, which almost starts a conversation about which superheroes are the coolest, which will sometimes start a conversation about what exactly makes a superhero. (These conversations with eighth graders would eventually lead me to create a whole unit on comic book superheroes for American Lit in high school, since I argue that superheroes are just about the only literary convention Americans didn't steal outright from someone else.)

Shit. You see how easy I am to distract?

Anyway, we argued about superheroes one day, and someone argued that Batman wasn't a superhero because he didn't have a superpower.

"Yes he does," said a voice from the back, "his superpower is White privilege." So that's when I knew that Monica was going to be one of those kids I was going to love. For most of that year, Monica and her two friends were most of what kept me from quitting forever. They were smarter and funnier than eighth graders had any right to be, and we fast developed a relationship that allowed us to give each other shit nearly all the time, and then also talk about the real-deal stuff about life that made life hard.

I was very often their teacher, but I was sometimes just their friend, and it didn't really occur to me how big a problem that could be.

It was during one of those friend times when we were all sitting around my room eating lunch (them eating away from the food-throwing, that's-what-she-said world of middle school lunch and me away from the shade-throwing, did-you-hear-what-she-said world of the teachers' lounge). During the conversation, it came out that Monica was dating someone her mom didn't know about.

"But don't tell. You can't." She looked so seriously at me, seriously enough that I knew, of course, I had no other option but to call her mom and tell her because something was up.

"Sorry," I said, "I have to call your mom, because safety and stuff."

"If you tell, I swear to god I'm never talking to you again."

So that's where being too much a friend can get you. Students can try to leverage that friendship against the work you know you need to do. In that situation, it wasn't going to work, but I've watched (and been) that cool teacher who doesn't push too hard for kids who should really do their work. There was one teacher in my school who would send "Good morning" texts to a few of her students every day (ick), and I watched those students lose their goddamn minds whenever that teacher tried to hold the line with them on doing what they were supposed to do.

I called Monica's mom. Of course I did. Monica did talk to me again, but it did take a few months before she was all the way cool with me. That was almost a decade ago, and she still keeps in touch from New York, where she is kicking the ass of the whole damn world. We've both written letters recommending the other for whatever they needed recommending for, but the real respect we built and the real work and growth we shared was as teacher and student. Not being friends doesn't mean you can't care about your students, but it does mean you have to care about them enough that you can push them.

Real work gets done when you're not worried about total control and you get to a magical point in your life where the opinions of teenagers on your coolness is not of all-encompassing importance. What you really want as a teacher is for students to respect you, and real respect doesn't come from who yells the loudest or who sits backwards in a chair and talks about how all the other teachers are lame. Respect comes less from anything you will say, and more from how often you listen, really listen, to your students. When you can tune your ear right, they'll tell you exactly what they need from you.

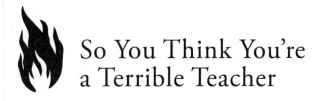

So You Think You're a Terrible Teacher

SO WE'RE A FEW WEEKS INTO SCHOOL NOW. Let me guess: you don't think it's going that well. You're through your first mini-unit, the one you planned over the last month of summer, and you're into your first round of lessons you planned the night before. Let me guess: it's not super smooth yet.

Your kids aren't listening, your kids aren't learning. Your kids aren't excited, your kids don't like you.

You are working as hard as you feel like a person can work, and things get better for a day, and then worse for a day, and then there's a day that's just kind of okay, and somehow that's worse. You feel like there's something you aren't doing that you should be doing, like there are things you do that you shouldn't, and if you could figure them out, everything would get better. You don't know what those things are.

So let me guess: you think you're a terrible teacher.

You might be.

Really, you might be. I don't know. I don't know you, and I've never watched you teach. You might just suck at this. You might want to figure out something else to do with your life. You felt like this was the only thing you were ever going to be really good at, and it turns out you suck. That has to hurt, but it's probably best to accept it, move on, maybe think about culinary school. That seems nice, too. Especially if you're a terrible teacher.

I doubt you are, though.

Really.

I don't think there are that many terrible teachers out there. I think most of those teachers think they're doing everything right anyway, which is why they're ultimately so bad. I think teaching is just really hard. In fact, I know that's true. Teaching is just really hard.

It's hard for everyone. It's even hard for people who are doing it well. It's especially hard for people who are doing it well. I've been teaching for longer than I've been doing any other thing in my life. I'm pretty cocky about it. I think I'm pretty damn good.

I'm through my first few weeks of my whateverth year of teaching, and want to know how it feels? It feels like my kids aren't listening, my kids aren't learning, my kids aren't excited, my kids don't like me. It feels like I'm a terrible teacher.

Why don't I act like it? I'm cocky. I'm stupid. I probably care less about a couple of bad weeks now that I've taught a few hundred weeks than I would have when I'd only taught just those first couple.

I'm not a terrible teacher. It feels like it sometimes, because every year is a new year. Every student is a student I haven't met before, even if I taught them last year. Every student is a mushy, messed-up human just like me, and we have to figure each other out for a while. Every year starts with new-year franticness, and sometimes what I'm teaching just doesn't rank compared to who's cute now, who's going out now, who's fighting, who's new, who's bi, who got into what trouble over the summer. Also, no matter what I do, some students aren't ever going to care a lot about school, which is probably because school is mainly just dumb stuff you have to do. Sometimes students are just Seniors. Still, I have them nearly an hour a day, and my constant lack of getting them to care makes me feel like a failure an hour a day.

But I know I'm not a terrible teacher, even though I fail at teaching pretty often. I know I'm not a terrible teacher. The test is easy, because I made the test up. Think you're a terrible teacher? Find out.

SO YOU THINK YOU'RE A TERRIBLE TEACHER: THE TEST.

(Check all that apply. You can check more than one.)

CATEGORY ONE

____ I don't care about teaching.

____ I don't care about students.

____ I like making people feel bad, especially young people.

____ I'm thinking about going into Administration.

CATEGORY TWO

____ I care about teaching.

____ I care about students.

____ I try hard.

____ I mess up, then try to figure out why.

____ I try to be interesting.

____ I try not to let myself feel too important.

____ I take breaks.

____ I apologize.

____ Sometimes, I wake up at three in the morning, and I can't go to sleep because I'm thinking about some awful thing I said or some hurtful thing a student said, and I think about what I could do the next day to make it better in some way.

____ I have fun.

____ I may carry grudges, but I try not to act like it.

____ I know at least three decent jokes.

____ I'm pretty smart.

____ I will go see student performances, even if it's choir or a musical.

____ I do no harm.

____ I do some harm, but I feel bad about it, and then try to fix it.

____ I try to keep things relevant, even when they aren't.

___ I see school through students' eyes sometimes.
___ I reflect.
___ I'm honest.
___ I'm respectful.
___ I'm trustful.
___ I'm realistic.

So are you a terrible teacher? Tally up your score and find out!

CATEGORY ONE: If you have checked any items in this category, you suck. Go do something else. Okay, fine, if you only checked the fourth but not the other three, be an administrator. Whatever.

CATEGORY TWO: Did you check the first two? Great. You're set. Three's not bad either. The rest of the things will probably help but are wildly biased toward my own brand of teaching.

TEACHING IS JUST REALLY HARD. You are working as hard as you think you are. You are holding yourself to an impossible and essential standard of success and you should keep doing that, but you should know that you're successful on levels you don't always see or know. Sometimes you'll feel like you suck, and sometimes you legitimately will.

Do you care? You'll be fine. Do you care a lot? You'll probably be great.

Part III

WINTER

In winter, I set my alarm earlier because it's going to be dark when I wake up no matter what. I get to school before almost everyone, make a pot of coffee, sit and look out the window, and feel warm and settled.

Winter is a time to take care of yourself, even when it's hard; to take care of your kids, because they make it hard; and to do the best, biggest, most fun things, because just making it out of bed is a pretty big deal.

The Goddamn Internet

I GRADUATED FROM HIGH SCHOOL IN 1999 with a GPA high enough for a four-year college, though not so high to get into a college that would impress anyone. To graduate high school successfully, I did many things that I found to be pointless, and I was pretty good at them. The smart kids remembered everything and were rarely asked to think about anything.

Seventeen years later, my education is relevant for little other than Trivia Night. I don't blame my high school, though I greatly disliked it, because who then could have imagined the immediate and constant access to information we would soon have, access that put at our fingertips nearly everything the smart kids were rewarded for remembering? Still, that information is here, and until the zombie apocalypse kills us all (or at least our cell towers), the information isn't going away.

Schools are jumping all over the technology wave (only a decade or so after the wave crashed over everyone else, but still). Schools roll out new devices, digital tools, online communication, and increased access for students every year. Too often, though, new tools are being asked to fix old problems. Worse, still, we sometimes exclude technology from the classroom, forcing a tech-free zone that exists no other place in kids' lives. It's handy for us, because we can keep teaching the way we were taught, but I don't imagine it's particularly helpful for those students when they leave our rooms.

Late in my first year of teaching I was reading the book *Kaffir Boy*, an apartheid-era memoir, with my students. The book is long, detailed, and full of interesting and shocking stories. To help kids keep up with everything happening in the novel, and to separate the pages on the Soweto Riots from the pages on the layout of the family's third home, I had them keep chapter summaries in notebooks. Some students used multicolored Post-its: red for plot summary, yellow for individual people of importance, green for important or interesting quotes. It all felt very much like I must be teaching something pretty important and students must be learning. It was, after all, the exact sort of thing I had done, or pretended to get done, while I was in school.

Of course, I had little intention of ever reading through the volumes of summaries being hammered out by my students. I assigned the summaries as one of a few layers of threat to get them to read the book. There would also be quizzes, graded discussions, projects, and an essay final, all asking in one way or another, "Did you read it?"

Of course, it didn't occur to me the insult it is to children to assume they won't read a good book when given one, or that they should read a not-good book because we said so, or that writing short summaries and recalling inane details have anything to do with the way books as an art are to be explored and enjoyed.

Two years later, I was doing the same book in the same dumb way (mainly, I think, because I did it fourth quarter and meant to work on it during the school year and then I'd think, nah, I'll work on it over the summer for next year, then spent my summer biking, playing video games, and napping). By that third year, though, the students stopped complaining about the summaries. The summaries themselves, those I read, anyway, were longer and more detailed. I chalked up the improved quality of work to the two things I credited all year for the good things happening in my room: the kids all had laptops, provided by the school, that made work more efficient and more engaging to do; and I was in my third year and getting really damn good at my job.

While grading them, I came across a few sentences. Something about them, especially coming from an eighth grader, seemed almost poetic and certainly brilliant. "Does he want to die? The threats are real. A collection of short sentences, haiku-like and perfect, stood out as a great concise summary of a complex section."

"Man, these kids can write," I said to myself. (It may be that I'm the only one who will listen when I talk like this.) "Man," I continued to myself, "I can fucking teach." I immediately e-mailed the parents of that student to tell them how great their kid was at writing and reading (and to insinuate strongly that a very specific dude may well be the reason).

Then, in the second student's work, "Does he want to die? The threats are real . . . ."

"Ah," I said aloud, alone at my desk after finding those formerly brilliant words, many of the longer and better summaries of many of my students word for word on various websites, "the goddamn Internet."

Therein lies the dilemma with technology. The work can look better, be longer, more polished, more complete, and also still involve not a single moment of learning. I've taken to instituting a new policy in the work involved in my classes. A policy, or a rule, or . . . I suppose most accurately, a question: "Can Google do this?"

I try not to assign anything the Internet will do for the kids. The trick is to use the pervasiveness of technology and information as a plus. I can assume access to information, assume students can access dictionaries, spellcheck, SparkNotes, Wikipedia, and move forward past the things those websites take care of. They know all that or know where to find all that. So what next? What's further?

This year, I applied the question to *Othello,* a text similar to *Kaffir Boy* in a few important ways. Students found the prose of each to be difficult to access while finding the subject matter to be pretty engaging. There was also a wide variety of previously written summaries, essays, and analyses of both spread liberally around the Internet. Asking students to prove they read either would ultimately be a test of whether or not they could type the name close enough into a search engine for it to guess correctly ("*Athelo* . . . did you mean *Othello?*").

We wrapped our study of *Othello* around issues of race and gender, most especially on how each is used to cast characters as "other" to their detriment. So, gone are the days of chapter summary. Our first-week assignment involved taking key terms from the sociological discussion (*dehumanization, misrepresentation, marginalization, normalization*), finding definitions online, synthesizing them into a definition in the student's own words, and including an example from the modern world and two illustrative quotes from the first three scenes of the play (read in class). Will Google do all that? Not all of it, no. Will it help? If you use the Internet well, read closely, and think, it will help. That's what I was looking for.

The first assignment was a building block. I did not want to move forward with discussions where our key words were tossed around without the students mutually understanding them. The assignment is a little more worksheety than I like to get, a little easier to copy than I would hope, but I used class time to engage with the students in their work, answering their questions, and to push their thinking. (This strategy is called teaching. Lots of people do it.) By the end of the week, I heard students remark that they were being dehumanized by the dress code and marginalized by the seating trends in the lunchroom. So I knew they were ready to move on.

The next assignment asked students to pick any group that is marginalized. Students picked lots of different groups: women in video games and superhero comics, Black women in reality TV, police officers, Muslims, victims of abuse, guns rights advocates, gay teens, and horror movie characters. Quite a few students latched on to the current discussion around Native mascots in professional sports, "because it's racist." The project reflected the diverse experiences and interests of the students, and I rarely had to say no or redirect an idea, which helped prove a point—that lots of humans treat other humans horribly. To prove their point, students used the Internet to look at lots of different kinds of media that involved their group; to discover patterns and evidence; to read and analyze media as text and sociological artifact.

The project had two goals. The first was to push the kids to disassemble and analyze things and discuss them intelligently. I told them it just wasn't powerful or interesting to say that the Washington Redskins' name is racist, but it was both powerful and interesting to be able to explain why. So they went and figured out a bunch of why. Plus, taking away phones and blocking websites does very little to curb Internet bullying or any of the other ickies kids use the Internet for, but teaching them empathy and literacy and basic "Don't be an asshole" skills does a lot.

The second goal was approached through a creative project after the analysis. Students created a counterstory to the things they found. This is where things got especially good. One student's idea was to rework the then-logo of the University of North Dakota's Fighting Sioux to a "Fighting Sue" logo of an angry-looking old lady. The student explained, "It's supposed to offend old White people. It's satire." So many magic words. A+, young friend.

Other students wrote treatments for shows that included characters of color with more depth and complexity. One student came in, I kid you not, with a poster board (presumably bought at Woolworth's or a Ben Franklin store in southeastern Wisconsin), with glue and paper, squiggly designs and all, that included facts and milestones of five people's lives, the words SUCCESSFUL STRIPPERS plastered across the top layered with neon green and pink letters.

In the meantime, we were still studying *Othello,* but almost none of that work went home with kids. The play, and what I wanted them to get from the play, did not pass the Google Test. I felt confident that most of any reading I assigned to most kids would result in a SparkNotes free-for-all to complete whatever comprehension assignment that went with it. I don't love that it's true, but I'm realistic that it's true. Kids, my kids anyway, enough of them to be a relevant number, won't read at home when there is another option. So we did that work together where I could control the pace, point out moments of great importance or relevance to our discussions (and the dirty jokes). I tried to make the funny parts funny and the villains infuriating. I did everything I could to make them, if not love *Othello,* at least understand why some people would. (This is also called teaching.)

So those are some days at their best: students using technology to find and reinforce knowledge, to study and discover how the world works while, and this was the trickiest bit, applying the knowledge and enthusiasm generated to experience a classic work of genius at a deeper level than simply reading it and watching the movie. The last part is challenging because, really, most kids would rather not. Kids love looking at the world around them, at TV shows they love and websites like Tumblr, which know them better than their parents. Getting students engaged in modern media is not a great challenge, but it's hard to avoid any media unit crawling so far up its own ass it doesn't know where it came from. (Make a logo that represents a feeling inspired by a product worn by a celebrity!)

The Google Test guides some pretty important things about my teaching. It helps me focus on teaching students skills they can apply broadly from my discipline instead of wasting my and my students' time on details of stories and memory tests. The Google Test asks, Will this help the student five years from now? Does it teach them to use technology or to learn on technology? Above all else, it helps me know that they are thinking.

AH, BUT WHAT ABOUT *THE* TESTS (bom-bom-BOM), the mandated soul-sucking, world-destroying tests? Shouldn't we be teaching to the tests so scores can go up? No, we should be teaching past the tests so scores can go up. My students, by being more engaged, by reading more deeply, by finding their own texts to investigate, are ultimately working far harder on core reading skills than they would be if I handed them a packet, but they don't realize it. I'm tricky.

In another project during the year, perhaps my very favorite project of the year, I teamed up with the World History teacher. Students picked a historic event from somewhere in the Middle East and learned a bunch about it. Many components of the project were similar to research projects and papers I've written and assigned in the past. There were a certain number of sources that had to be found, a general scope of the project to be adhered to, rubrics and checklists and due dates. It's the sort of stuff that every high schooler is doing in every high school, and also the sort of stuff that doesn't often pass the Google Test.

Our twist, and it proved to be an important twist, was in the final product. For a research project like this, students would normally write an essay with all their information, and you know what? A lot of them would do a pretty good job. The A's from the project would be solid A's involving writing and rewriting, hours and hours and then some hours of hard work, a solid ratio of one mental breakdown for every five White girls in the room, and an essay that even the teacher won't read every word of.

The real problem is in the D's of the project. The D's will be poor D's. Students will write things without really knowing. Students will cheat—you and I both know that they will. Many D's, in fact, will ride a fine line between plagiarism and summary, and many will jump the line with both feet and hope for the best.

And who can blame them? As an English teacher, I started my career with a distressing reverence for the essay. It was, so far as I could tell, the height of all things in our craft, the catch-all assessment. Kids who could write good essays were good at English, and kids who couldn't, weren't. I ignored the fact that I had skated through many literature classes learning nothing and reading less because I could write one hell of a bullshitting essay and could write them long enough to be sure my teachers wouldn't read enough to know.

After school ends, all but a small fraction of people will ever write an essay again. That's because essays aren't all that important anywhere but middle school, high school, or college. What's important, it turns out, are many, but not all, of the things that essays are good for. Essays show that you read something and thought about it, that you synthesized information, that you can make and support a good argument, that you can express your emotions and intents and beliefs to other people. They show all those things, which are important things. They also show how well you can use a certain dialect of English to write in very certain sorts of ways. So I assign essays sometimes when I want to test all those things. I don't assign them when I want to just focus on the first batch, the skills I think are the most important for my students moving forward. My students get lots of ways to show me they know English, even the ones who can't write for crap.

For our research assignment, we did graphic novels. Students had to research and turn that information into something that could be drawn, a story that could be told. The key words were *synthesize* and *humanize*.

Oh my god, some of them were awful. Stick figures, half drawn in pen and half in pencil. Misspellings galore. Stories that lacked most, or any, of the components of what a story should be. A few projects approached a sort of sick, brilliant, befuddling cross between a collage, a science project panel board, and a stream of consciousness acid-trip poem. Projects were the victims of wasted work hours and hurried completion. The beautiful wreckage of poorly applied pencil and potential.

Those were the D's. The glorious D's. I was so proud of them. They were, without rival, the best group of D work I had ever received in my life. Why? Because there was nothing about those final products that could be Googled, nothing that could be copy and pasted. Before you could draw a crummy picture, you had to at least have an idea of what that crummy picture should be of. It frustrated the hell out of some kids, kids who begged me to just let them do an essay. They didn't want to have to make something. So there were D's, furiously spectacular D's, but there were no F projects. F projects were impossible, because the students had to do something, had to learn something in order to turn something in. The D's were good D's.

There were also lots of A's, lots of projects that showed a

great amount of effort, thought, planning, and talent. They were better than essays because they were human. They were focused on people, on the experience of people, but were human especially because the personality of the students came through in what they wrote and drew. They read, researched, and thought, and those A projects took all that actual analysis and synthesis and made a whole brand new thing out of it. The A's were very good A's.

But then there were the ultra A's. There were two or three assignments that were in the upper echelon of things I've ever had turned in to me in all my years of teaching. There was one that was one of the best works of art I've ever seen. That project, a study of the wall that divides Israel and Palestine through the graffiti on each side, took two students just a shade over three months to finish. There were binders of research that went into making the four-page story, cut down the middle by the wall, of a young Palestinian and young Israeli person sneaking to the wall at night to create artwork that spoke of hope and beauty. It will be a portfolio piece for art school applications. It will hang on my wall for as long as I have a classroom.

It turns out, and I should have known it, that kids will often do nothing if you let them, and kids will often make something brilliant if you give them the chance.

This is perhaps the real goal of the Google Test: to make more makers. We need students who are not just able to read, not just read and remember, and not just read, remember, and analyze. Those are all handy skills but are all mostly passive skills. We need to make more makers, students who don't just understand problems but show they understand them by creating new and novel solutions. We need students who don't just read and remember, but who learn in order to do.

The Worst
Advice Ever

IN SOME SCHOOLS, the sky falls down about once every ten years. These are the schools where outside forces move slowly, and new projects are introduced only when a committee about a committee has been approved to work toward the formation of a task force and everyone decides to move forward. In those schools, it will feel like the sky is falling, like life and school will never be the same, like any chance at success you may have been grasping at will be gone by next year, leaving behind only smoking wreckage and a postapocalyptic landscape of students asked to write using only their own saliva and reading out of textbooks written only in corporate-logo letters. These are the lucky schools, those that have years off from this feeling, and I do not work in a lucky school. In my school, the sky is perpetually falling down.

The first time my school was supposed to end forever there was some small amount of drama involving parent protests, letter writing, and speech giving. Things almost, but not quite, got to the level of button making. Buttons were threatened.

A well-meaning teacher, one who had sort of appointed himself my mentor because he really liked hearing himself talk (I'm that guy now), pulled me aside one day. He put a hand on my shoulder and said, "When I was a young teacher, my department chair pulled me aside, just like this, and he gave me the best piece of advice I ever got." It was all very serious and dramatic. Some day, young Simba, all that the sun touches will be yours.

"'Close the fucking door,' he said. He said, 'Close the fucking door.'"

He went on from there, for quite some time, really, about all the reasons to ignore everything around you and just teach your class. Just close the door, do your thing, shut the rest out. It sounded a lot like really great advice.

It was the absolute worst advice I've ever received. Simba, screw everyone else, go find a comfy bed, and hang out. Simba, you can only worry about what you can change, and you can't change much.

Friends, young friends, do not close your doors. Do not. It is not good for your school; it is not good for your room, for your kids, or for you. Open your doors, go forth. Go forth and make messes and build things and throw your voice into problems and places where it is not asked. Go, go, go.

Go, because teaching is a team sport, because what you experience within your room should matter deeply to those outside of it, and what happens outside of school is hugely important to how things go in your room. Teaching can be too lonely and it can be too easy to imagine you are the only one struggling or the only one getting it right, and neither of those things is ever true. Get out of your room. Talk to teachers about teaching, talk to them about students. Look from as wide a lens as you can manage at the issues that shape school, and throw your energy and experience into making them better.

YOUR BUILDING

It should go without saying that you should be involved in your building, but it turns out that it has to be said. I've worked with teachers who, halfway through the school year, couldn't tell me the names of anyone who worked in the office, where the computer lab was (or who ran it), or the names of any teachers who didn't share a lunch hour with them.

Look, there's an absurd amount of work to do, most especially in your first or second year, but meeting the people you work with and building connections with them will help you get that work done better and more easily. Promise.

There are lots of good ways to get involved in your building, even if you are relatively introverted (it's pretty fascinating how many teachers are zany maniacs in front of a group of children but can't seem to get a word out of their mouths in a staff meeting). If you drink, go to happy hours. If you don't drink but can go to happy hours and order a soda and some fries, do that. Time outside of the room, outside of the building, away from the eyes of parents, students, and bosses is absolutely essential. Sure, happy hours can help you find new friends in your building, but it can also help smooth out relationships with people who you generally want to hit in the head with a desk.

Teaching is important, and teaching feels important, and so it can feel really important during the day when someone takes the computer lab without signing it out correctly, or plans a hallway activity in front of your door without asking. On Wednesday, that person can feel like your enemy, or like an enemy to all that is good in the world, an enemy on the level of Sauron, or Ultron, or man buns. Over a beer on Friday, it can seem kind of funny, and getting to know each other better will lessen the chances of violence on Monday, when they do the same damn thing again after you just told them not to, please.

If you're not the happy hour type, then quit. Get out. No one wants you here anyway, so you will fail, miserable and alone. Kidding. Jokes.

If you're not the happy hour type (and loath though I am to admit it, there is some argument to be made that watching your coworkers get drunk enough to make any number of verbal, emotional, or physical humiliations may not directly serve the best interests of professional relationships), don't make a lack of happy hours be the reason you don't get to know anyone.

If there are meetings, go to meetings. Listen at first if you aren't confident in saying what you think. If work comes up during those meetings, get involved in that work. Supporting other people's ideas is a great way to get involved, build some allies, and, as a happy by-product, probably get some work done that helps your school run better.

Support, by the way, means doing a lot more than saying, "Hey, great idea!" Lots of people will say that, even when they think someone else's idea is shit, but teachers need support on a much deeper level than reassurance. Look around your school for the best things happening and find out what help they need. When there are events, put your face there. When chaperones are asked for, put your body there. Throw some of your minutes at some problems, because minutes are the things that everyone ultimately needs more of. They will appreciate your minutes, and when you've got an idea that deserves some attention, you are far more likely to get it. Oh, and don't wait to have those ideas, and don't hesitate to speak boldly and bluntly when you feel like you should.

Because here's the beautiful and awful and poetic thing about teaching. While teaching, you will have the exact job title in your first year as you do in your last. I like that. It means, it should mean anyway, that you have exactly as much right to speak and be involved in your first year as you do in your twentieth. Just as experience should be listened to, so should the fresh perspective of a teacher early in their career. Anyone who makes you feel otherwise should be kicked in the shin with pointy shoes.

YOUR UNION

It's possible you will work in a building that is not in a union. In that case, in my expert opinion, you will not be able to become involved in your school union. If you do work in a building with a union, join that union. That's the first step. Some places are better than others at finding you and helping you sign up, but be prepared to ask around until you find the sheet you need and get it filled out. Also, understand that filling out that sheet is not involvement. Wearing the right T-shirt on the right day is not involvement. At that point, all you've done is given your money away and looked like a nerd at the grocery story after work. It is not involvement.

Your union is the primary voice of the teachers in your school and district. If your union is doing things you don't like, or speaking in a voice that is not yours, you have two choices: you can choose to not be involved, which is, I suppose, a thing. Before you do that, you may want to ask yourself what good not being involved will do. You may feel justified in the midst of your own personal movie that no one is watching. You may feel as if you have taken a stand and cleared your conscious of your membership supporting something you don't like. Yep. But then what?

The fuck-the-system teenager in me hates that I have come to this point, but I think it's often more powerful and productive to work from inside systems than it is to stand outside and throw stones.

It took me a few years to get really involved in my local union. I went to meetings and kept my mouth shut, worried that the thoughts of a young teacher meant nothing in a room of experienced union hard-asses. I heard enough of, "We've always done . . ." and "When you're here long enough, you'll know . . ." to know somewhere deep down that I was expected to learn and not do, not yet.

A few years in, I was much more comfortable in my skin and had begun to take on leadership roles in my school, but I still felt out of my depth when contracts and teacher rights were discussed. At the first big union meeting of the year (a month after we were supposed to have it, always), about halfway through the usual routine of eating through the president's report, a new teacher spoke up.

"I came today to ask for help," he said, "because I don't know how else to get it." He was a first-year social studies teacher who continued by rattling off a long list of extra jobs outside of teaching he had been asked to do so far that year. There were dances, performances, a lock-in, additional meetings, setting up events, staffing events, cleaning up events, all that he felt he as an untenured first-year teacher (which is a bit like being a turtle without a shell) could not say no to. He was exhausted and struggling to find the time and energy he needed to devote to actually teaching and learning to teach better.

"I couldn't help notice," he said as he held his palms out, apologizing, "that it's mostly new teachers doing all those things, and I think it would be really helpful if everyone pitched in so it didn't always fall on us." He was right. I'm sure it happens in many schools that teachers work like crazy during their first few years taking on extra responsibilities. I did. During my first few years I acted as a coach, a chaperone, and an event planner. I worked constantly and nearly let stress drive me out of the classroom at least a dozen times.

The vice president of our union answered him, quite matter-of-factly, "Just wait till you get tenure, and you can stop doing all the extra stuff." She was right. You kind of can. I mean, you can so long as you don't care about the people you work with. No one's going through due process to fire a teacher because they didn't come to the eighth grade dance or stay at the end of open house to fold tablecloths. I've done a little less, if I'm going to be honest, as I've gone through the years. I've stopped making sure I'm there for all of everything, have picked and chosen a little more, and let other people pick up my slack.

It's an awful, awful thing we do, and we shouldn't. Presumably, as you work longer at being a teacher, you become better at teaching. The job becomes less stressful and, especially if you are teaching the same subject for many years in a row, the job becomes less work. People always blanch at being told they are doing less, because it always feels like you are doing a lot, but in my first few years I had to create everything I used in my class. Every lesson plan, every assignment, every presentation. As the years went on, I would add and tinker all the time, but I had many many things that I got to use again without thinking about for longer than five minutes.

I had never spoken up at a union meeting until that moment, but that first-year teacher needed someone to tell him different. I asked if we, as a union and professional organization, could do more to push our teachers to help out. I asked if we could start a movement to help support our newer teachers in more ways. I was told, much as the other teacher was, that the first years just suck, and everyone had to go through it. Someone actually used the phrase *sink or swim,* and I threw a piece of bowling-alley pizza at their face. I think that happened (it didn't).

That year, I ran for my first union position. In the years that followed, I was a constant nagging voice bringing things to the union that were different from what they had done, that were on my mind specifically because I had not been around for long enough. I don't say this to brag about my own awesomeness. My only special skill, if I have one, is the ability to keep talking even when everyone at a table is looking at me like I'm an idiot. (Have I mentioned that I'm a White man?)

If you've gone to a few local meetings, and just don't feel your time is being well spent, look for other levels of involvement. State organizations often feel and act much differently from local ones, and there are usually ways to get involved at a state level that the crankies in your local cannot stand in the way of. Look for trainings, town halls, or open meetings being held at your state union and get involved.

My state holds a summer program for a few days on a campus in the middle of nowhere. You get three days of a dorm bed and meals for eighty bucks, and you can go get drunk at night with everyone at the American Legion for seven bucks. It was my first year at that summer program that led to my going to several national events (Oh, you want to pay to fly me to Vegas in January? Okay.), joining a committee to increase the engagement and strength of newer union members, and being convinced that change can come to and through our union.

My involvement in my union—local, state, and national— has given me a chance to add my voice to the most powerful collective voice that teachers have. I've watched lots of things I don't like, and a few things I couldn't be more proud of, which is, I think, what real work looks like most of the time.

ACTIVISM

This year a student was missing from my classroom. He wasn't sick, wasn't absent, but he wasn't there. The thing is, I really needed him in my room that day, and he wasn't there. The attendance program on my computer was showing nothing, and none of his friends seemed to know where he went. "He was just behind me." "Peeing?" "Maybe a girl talked to him." "Yeah, right."

I got class started and called to the office.

"Hey, I'm having trouble finding Josh." (Josh sometimes has trouble finding where he is supposed to be.)

"We've got him." (Sometimes he wanders to the office to chat with whoever's in trouble outside, because they often have the best stories.)

"Oh. Okay, is he on his way then?" (And sometimes they just need to remind him that, you know, class started ten minutes ago.)

"He's being sent home. He'll be back Friday" (Oh. Okay.)

"Oh shit, Josh got suspended." The voice was from one of Josh's friends. Texts travel faster than light. A few minutes later, the attendance was updated, and there, right next to Josh's name: "Suspension."

We got the whole story as the hour unfolded. Josh was wearing a hat in the hallway and was told by a staff member to take the hat off.

"Why?" (It's a good question, when you think about it.)

"Because it's a school rule." (Not a good answer.)

"That's dumb." (It is.)

"Take it off. Now. Or I'm taking it from you." (Also dumb.)

"Fucking bullshit." (Not strategically great, though a poetically compelling statement.)

Both people involved in the conversation had voices raised by the end. The staff member was, I'm sure, just trying not to spend a long time enforcing a rule and was upset at anything but immediate compliance. Josh can get loud and mad, especially when someone is coming at him in a way he sees as rude, and nothing says rude like demanding immediate compliance.

Josh was sent to the office, already heated. When he walked into the admin's office, she continued right where the staff member left off.

"Sit down. Now." (She stands up.)

"No." (He stands still.)

"I don't like your attitude." (She steps forward.)

"That's because this is fucking bullshit." (He stands still.)

"Language!" (She points her finger.)

"Fuck this." (He walks out; he gets suspended.)

I'm on Josh's side here, and not just because I needed Josh in class. From his perspective, he was just walking down the hallway and he got hassled about a dumb hat (no doubt with four other kids wearing hats within sight). Then, for no real good reason (swearing is a lot less a big deal to some people, and Josh is one of those people), Josh is sent to the office, where he is treated like he just punched a puppy, and then he is sent home for three days for calling bullshit on some bullshit. Nothing, it should be noted, or hardly ever anything, is ever said to the adults along the way who escalated the student to the point of his snapping.

From their point of view, the actions of the staff members involved are simple to understand. If we let kids get away with hats, there would be no order. If we let kids get away with swearing, there would be chaos. If we let kids call bullshit, there will be riots. Riots!

Or maybe just people get tired, and they find it's a lot easier to say that kids come first than it is to really treat them like they do.

If Josh were the first or the only, I likely would have been content to write a vague, snarky Facebook post about the incident and move on with my life. Josh wasn't the first, not even a little bit. I had noticed the pattern in my room of students being sent home for things like "disrespect" and "insubordination." Sometimes loudness was being read as threatening, and sometimes quietness was being treated as an admission of guilt.

Suspensions were conditioning my students to see themselves as bad kids. They were not reforming behavior: they were undercutting a community of building respect based on relationships and supplanting them with a community of acting like you respect people or else. Plus, Josh wasn't in my class, and I really needed him in class that day. Every day he's not in class is a day I can do very little for him. I need my kids in class. Even, in fact, especially those students who are having trouble staying in school.

I want the kids in my room, and I want them all there. The kids getting sent home are disproportionately Black and Brown kids, and they're getting sent home for not fitting into a White and White system. I want them in my room so they can show me where that system needs pushing and call me on my shit, and because it's absolutely criminally stupid that we haven't figured out yet how to serve them better.

I want the kids in my room because it's their right to be there. Schools aren't built for me to have a nice day: they are built to create opportunities for kids, to discover and expand talent, to give tools for all the work our students may someday do. These are the things we can't do without kids in the room.

I want the kids in my room now, and if we're sending them home for being disrespectful, we should be ashamed of ourselves for not earning their respect. If a student is having a problem, and the problem only escalates as we intervene, we should not be suspending that student: we should be taking a hard look at our interventions. Sending them home is the easy way out for the day but builds nothing for their return.

Josh was the catalyst that got me reading about suspensions and finding that I was actually pretty late to the party. There were a few hardworking groups in my area already publicly pushing for an end to nonviolent suspensions. I liked those groups on Facebook, and I felt pretty good about myself. The next week, another kid got suspended, and I started reading every article those groups posted on Facebook, even taking the step of liking each one of those statuses. So, you know, I was getting pretty badass.

In a conversation with a teacher at another school, I brought up suspensions, and she told even more striking tales of tomfoolery and shitheadery at her school. That day, a leader from one of the regional groups sent out an invite for a group. I went. I raised my hand, I committed to action, and I took my first steps toward working as an advocate for my students and colleagues outside of my own school building.

Suspensions may not be your thing, but whatever your thing is, I can almost assure you that there is a group working on it somewhere. Look for groups that are working on what you care about, because those groups are looking for you. If there isn't one, you can start one, and you should. You should because just like it's crucial to your students what the teacher in the room next to you is doing, it is important to your school what the schools around you are doing. So it's important to get involved outside of your school.

Advocacy is also supremely energizing. Many teachers I know have shied away from the step outside of their school because it feels like "one-more-thing." We work hard. Of course we do. It's hard to imagine putting in hours doing anything more than we are doing. I get that. But we are used to the one-more-things that come from our schools, and those things are often tiring for the exact same reasons the rest of our day is tiring, and we are often at our limit for that specific brand of tiring. Those arguing against engaging at a broader level are missing out on a very important thing: when you do work outside of your school, no one knows your assistant principal.

I've been hard on admin so far in this section, which is not my general approach to my bosses, but hear me out on this point. Even when your administrators are good, teachers often spend their time with each other bitching about them. Why? Because no one likes being told what to do, and no one likes being told they can't have everything they want. And who in the building is often most responsible for delivering those messages? Well, your principal is often busy that day, so your assistant principal will likely be the one sending the "Stop by my office" e-mail.

When we are with teachers from our own buildings, even (or especially) at union meetings, we often talk about small problems. Those small problems can be really important, but no one gets into teaching to fight for a five-minute-longer lunch break. No one believes the purpose of education is to minimize the travel time and noise of students between rooms, and when you work with teachers or advocates away from your building, you will quickly find that no one cares how those things are going in your building.

Big groups deal with big problems, and being a part of them can keep you centered on the real reasons you wanted a classroom in the first place. They can be something that actually takes some one-more-things off your plate because they help you see that a whole lot of them aren't that important to you. They can also help challenge another popular saying among teachers: that you should only worry about what you can change. Teachers, and probably normal people too, use the phrase "You can only worry about what you can change" as an excuse to not work on plenty of very changeable things. What they mean, whether they understand they mean it or not, is, "I don't want to worry about things I don't feel like putting the work in to change." But who wants to be that person, really?

We can't do it all, and certainly not by ourselves. The great thing is, we don't need to. I know this one guy who is an absolute ed nerd. He loves policy and meetings and everything else awful in the world. We both agree that we're at A and need to move to Z. His work is all about moving A to B to C, while my work is often about stomping my feet and yelling that we need to be at Z three decades ago. I like to think of him as an education professional and myself as an education activist. (I often think of myself as having cooler descriptions than the people around me, but he's also a foot and a half taller than I and blisteringly attractive, so he can handle it.) The thing is, I need him. We're never getting to Z without some persistent, progressive change in that direction. The other thing is, he needs me. We're never moving past C if there's not yelling and stomping about how much further we have to go. We each do our work; we each work where we are most comfortable and effective. When things are working best, we are doing our work together.

The really important things, the really big important things, the things that make teaching the hardest and best job in the world, are things that teachers can change. We can't change them by tomorrow, and can't change them alone, and can't change them without a whole lot of work and stress and loudness, but we can change them—if we show up to try.

White-Guy Bullshit

"BITCH."

This was the intro to the term *dehumanization* for my tenth graders (who would spend much of the rest of World Literature talking about the ways writing and words are used to dehumanize people and groups of people, and how they can also be used to humanize).

We were reading a short story by Chimamanda Ngozi Adichie about two women, a Christian and a Muslim, trapped in a room during a religious riot. Dehumanization is the kind of concept that takes months to really land with students. This story is the kind of story that gets referred back to for months. I wanted kids to start to kick around the idea of having humanity, of what it means to be recognized as fully human, and then, the way that that humanity can be minimized, dismissed, or removed. It is many big thoughts.

After giving a very simple definition of *dehumanization,* I opened the floor for examples.

"The Holocaust."

Yep. That's always the first example: it gives me a chance to say my thing, which is, "No human has ever purposely hurt another human." What I mean is that in order for any of the small or large harms in human history to have occurred, someone had to be viewed as less than human.

Again, though, that's something I throw out there over and over, because I think it's the smartest thing I say.

Then, there's a pause. "Bitch."

Bitch is almost always the second example that students come up with when we talk about dehumanization. Their *why* is almost always the same, too: "Because it means female dog." (See? Because dogs aren't human.) I often let kids kick and claw their way through *bitch* for a while, and they often come to some really interesting definitions of the word. They figure out that when someone is called a bitch, it really has nothing to do with dogs. One group one year came up with, "an un-ideal woman," which is interesting, and another expanded that to "an un-ideal person of your gender," which is kick-a-chair insightful. This year a student said, "A woman who isn't acting like a man wants her to." Bam. Kids are smart. Plus, now we're talking about dehumanization as something a lot more complex than calling someone an animal.

But those are the ends of long conversations, conversations that are given time and space and are conducted in a place that is safe for those participating. On the day I'm thinking of, the day just after the Adichie story, the conversation took one of the sharp turns that conversations can take: the "I don't think people should be offended by that" discussion. That discussion, often introduced and pushed by a person sitting in privilege, and today offered by a student whose name was something like Jiggy or Boff or something you would name the sidekick friend in an '80s movie, is an often necessary piece in unearthing the difference between speaking to people and speaking for people.

But on the day that I'm thinking of, I didn't feel like I had that kind of time. We were a day away from an extended break, and I had a very specific goal for the lesson, so instead of doing something smart, I did something dumb.

When this student, Jiggy or Rootie (or whatever), carefree and sure of his world-dominating brilliance in a way that males often seem to be (cough-me-cough), began to speak for the women in the room, he explained to them that they shouldn't be offended by the word *bitch* because . . . (whatever) reasons. Another student, Liz, fierce and well-armed in a way that females seem to have to be (and never seem to be in movies that dudes like Rootie are in), let him have it, calling him out on his privilege, on the misogyny implicit in a man telling women what they should think and why.

I said, "You both have good points, and both should listen to each other, and I totally get how it seems like the intent of what you say should matter and be important, and there are totally situations where *bitch* is used where it is acceptable and a really nuanced conversation about this would allow for our ability to see things differently, and really all this needs to be later, later, and we'll get there, I promise, but we can't get there now, but sometime, for sure, we'll get there."

So, essentially, I said, "Wordsy words words, boys get to say what they want, angry girls get shut down, I'm important, blahblahblah, look at my stupid sport coat."

You know how the last thing you can say to an angry person that is helpful is "You should calm down"? That's pretty much what I did, and it was a dumb thing. When the class discussion broke up, I went over to Liz, a student I had known for four years, a student whom I had supported in a thousand ways, a student who, when I walked over, said, "Get away from me."

"Really? It's like that?"

"Really. It is."

So now I was pissed, and Liz was very opposite of calm. My student added a healthy dose of betrayal to her feelings of anger because I was not supposed to be that teacher. I always said I wasn't that teacher. I was rewarded constantly as not that teacher, and I was being that teacher and silencing her justifiable anger in favor of the comfort of the kid who just said a bunch of offensive shit.

I know all this because we both calmed down enough to go talk in the hallway, and she said, "You're supposed to be the teacher who doesn't do that and you did that. You were silencing my justifiable anger in favor of the comfort of the kid who just said a bunch of offensive shit." She was super right, and I was being an asshole. I let her know by saying, "You're super right, and I'm being an asshole." Sometimes I swear at school and nothing bursts into flames.

It turned out that Liz had seen a lot of things along the way, things I had screwed up, things that had centered male voices in the room and allowed some pretty awful things to be said in the name of honoring perspectives. She had let a lot of them slide or, rather, swallowed them and let me keep thinking I was being super great when I was really perpetuating a lot of the stuff in the exact moments I thought I was working against it. I was the best bet she had during her day, and she had been burned by people who react poorly at getting called on their shit.

She let it all out then, there in the hallway. She cut me off at the knees and told me that I thought I had this radically social justice classroom and, really, I just used the words a lot. Then she said, "Okay. Thanks for listening to that," and then she left.

I spent the long weekend reflecting on all of that. I was sure I had messed up, but I wasn't sure exactly how to do things better. Funny thing was that during that long break I was on my way to a conference on racial equity and, in a way that is not common in my life, found myself for days and days sitting and thinking hard about being not just a guy, but a White guy, and realizing that no matter how hard I tried, I would always be a White guy standing in front of the classroom, and it was past time I understood exactly what that meant.

So it was that four days later I was sitting with a group of White men.

As a White male, sitting in a group of White men is not an abnormal experience for me. Really, it's something I do just about every day. What was different about this group was that we were sitting together specifically because we were White men, because we were White men at a racial equity conference in a session about the intersections of race and gender, and because we were told to sit with people who identified as our same race and gender, because there are few things as uncomfortable for White people than pointing out the Whiteness of a whole bunch of White people.

So I was in this group, this White male group, and we were assigned the task of describing what it means to be White and male. It was a challenge. We wrote the words we knew we were supposed to write, since we had all been in enough conversations about race to know the right answers. We wrote *empowered* and *intelligent* and *fixers* and *holders of knowledge*. Tucked-in polo shirt guy said, "I don't like that everything on this list is negative."

So. Let that sink in a little bit. So reflexive was our guilt that our list of words was viewed as negative rather than as privilege. Shit.

We kept going, but the group began to bristle at every new addition, and before long the frustration spilled over enough to effectively derail the exercise. "I don't identify with that word," we started to hear, and as the "Not me," and the "That's not universal experience" and the "I don't think all of us" comments began to bump out the conversation, it started to sound all too familiar. "Not all men," we were saying, "not all White men." We were, as the most dominantly represented group in the country, unwilling to accept the idea that we were in fact a group.

Teachers, of course, do this. Especially White teachers. We struggle to understand that we are not just a White teacher in the front of the room but *another* White teacher in the front of the room.

ONE DAY I had a student, Mo, who was late to class for what felt like the bagillionth day in a row. After a warning, I demanded we make a call home together so his mom knew what was up, and he blew the fuck up. There was some yelling (from both), a healthy smattering of swear words (not from me, I don't swear when I'm angry), and suddenly we were ten or so minutes into class without a single bit of teaching and a student who was obviously, physically upset. To recap: in order to try to start class and learning on time, I tried something that resulted in all students starting class much, much later and directly and negatively affected the learning of the student I was addressing.

I'm not always very good at this.

When things calmed, I sat near Mo in a space away from other kids. Both of us were still pretty heated and trying hard to make the other person hear us without trying very hard to hear each other. He said, "Man, I just think sometimes that all White teachers are racist, and all I have is White teachers."

So I stopped my rant and heard that.

White teachers: I know few things for sure, and when conversations about race are happening, specifically when one of your students of color is talking to you about their experience, it is your job to stop teaching and listen. Don't rationalize, don't defend. Just shut up a minute and hear what they are telling you.

So I listened.

I heard that this student has seven classes a day, and all are taught by White people. I heard that this was the second year in a row that this was true. "It's just too many White people," I heard. I heard that the person in the building this student was most comfortable talking to was a substitute teacher, a Black male, who is here once or twice a week. "I tell him everything," I heard. I heard this student feels constantly singled out, treated unfairly, is called out when White kids are doing the same things, and that it's always been like this. Year after year, class after class, it's been like this.

So it is no wonder that in my and most classes, that when there is time to work and time to choose where to sit, my Black students sit together. It is often treated as a negative. Why are all the Black kids sitting together?

There are assumptions about the dangerousness or volatility of Black students occupying the same space. Walk through a school and look into classes with seating charts. Notice, specifically, where Black males are seated in relation to each other. Watch the assumption when a group of Black students working are assumed to be wasting time, especially when their focus and engagement may be reflected in louder ways than a group of White students working (or quietly disengaged). These are things I enforce when I am not thinking.

Surrounded by Whiteness in rooms very often led by White

people, my students create Black space during work time. My job is to let them.

If that doesn't make sense, think of it this way: as teachers, we are surrounded all day by students. That's okay. It's not like we hate students, but it can be a bit exhausting to be around them all day, to change the way we speak and our mannerisms to be able to communicate more effectively with them. So when it is time for supervision at the end of the day, and there are tons of kids running around, teachers will often congregate together. They create teacher space, where they can talk about being a teacher and can speak and act freely, where they can just fucking breathe for a second.

There are signs that the students are not fully comfortable with the space and culture of my room. I own that. I work on that. I can also give them room, make sure that I am not parking myself by the Black kids to redirect any talk or off-task moments while the White kids in the room are on Tumblr or drawing *Dr. Who* fan art free from harassment. I can understand and encourage the academic, emotional, and social support our kids of color are giving each other instead of wringing my hands about "that group over there" and all the work I assume they aren't doing. I can build room and reason and direction for Black and Brown spaces in my room and in my practice.

The interactions with Liz and Mo are not isolated. The interactions in our classrooms never are. I am not just a teacher: I am a White teacher, and my interactions are weighted with the interactions of other White teachers my students have had. Of all the privileges of being White and being male, the most powerful and seductive is that we are, each of us, a complete and human and individual person whose actions and beliefs operate independently of any other person on the planet. We are, each of us in our own ways, unwilling to commit to what it means to be part of the group we are sitting in, unwilling to accept the responsibility and reality of being a member of that group.

I've been watching in conversations around me and online as White people, especially White males, are denying the perspectives of people of color, are speaking over and through the voices of women, of anyone suggesting that either "White" or "male" is a group to say, "It offends me that you don't see each of us as individuals," as if the narratives told about people of color and women don't constantly treat them as a homogeneous identity. I watch as White people, especially White males, say that talking about race is what perpetuates racism. I watch as males, especially White males, threaten rape and murder to women who have spoken out about sexism (or spoken out at all, about just about anything). I've been thinking about how badly I don't want to be one of those guys, but how it's also really important for me to understand that, like it or not, the privilege those guys are so aggressively protecting is the same privilege I benefit from. It matters that I'm a White guy, and the reality of what that means matters every damn moment that I'm a White guy in a classroom.

I've been trying to figure out what the real answers should have been at the conference. When that group conversation started, a participant raised their hand and said, "How are we supposed to talk about race and gender when we're all White men?" So. Let that sink in, too. Let that sink in and think about how often panels on race and gender issues about non-White, non-male issues are being spoken to by White men. We are experts, apparently, on everything but what it means to be White and male.

I say "we" intentionally. I mean me. I mean all White people. If we are talking about those things, we need to talk about them more. We need to take responsibility for the fact that very few White people truly engage in the conversation, very rarely talk about race in spaces that are all White. We need to talk about race in groups of White people where it is uncomfortable to talk about them. We need to talk about them in staff meetings, not just Equity trainings. I'm saying *we* because it's uncomfortable for me to do. I so badly want to say, "Most, but not me, not all of us," but that's the problem, isn't it?

White-male privilege is not polite, is not sterile. It is a dangerous, messy, frighteningly powerful piece of my experience, of my daily teaching experience.

Don't think this doesn't happen in classrooms. From my

desk one day, I had a front-row seat to the damage that a well-meaning White guy can have while really thinking he's doing the right thing. This time, it wasn't me, which is why it was so much easier to see than all the screwing up I'd been doing.

A government class of seniors was in the hallway having a sort of circle conversation. Circles can be powerful and positive, a place where every voice is equal and equally included. This circle involved each student speaking until they said something that hit the play button on any number of the thousands of pre-programmed mini-lectures the teacher had at the ready. The students were talking about efforts that could be taken to improve police–community relations, and I could see where the teacher was coming from, trying to take a highly engaging real-world issue and bringing in student voices. Cool, except the teacher was doing 90 percent of the talking.

Problem was, in this circle conversation that wasn't, there was also a conversation about humanity that really could have been. After a "everyone say something they remember from yesterday" starter (Students: pass, pass, I dunno, pass, . . . umm . . . police? Teacher: YES! And wouldn't it be great if I recapped the whole lesson for you for ten minutes? Whee!), they started new material by defining *police brutality.* As a decent definition was constructed, one student interjected, "I'm so scared of police. I'm so scared of dying. I mean, I guess if a cop had their gun on me, I would just close my eyes and think of my family and hope that I died with dignity."

Ho-Lee-Shit.

This from a student who spent more time out of class than in, who spent more time in class nonsubtly referring to weed than actually referring to anything on topic. This from a student who wore class-clown status like a shield from sharing emotion. This from a young Black male, a student so much like so many faces that had become hashtags in the months and years before. This.

And then, from the teacher, "Okay, but Marcus, we're just on the definition now, so hold that thought." Then that. Hold that thought?

Marcus deflated, sat back in his seat, said nothing. Within

five minutes he was wandering toward the bathroom, then down the hall, then god-knows-where for the rest of the hour. His moment of honesty, of incredible vulnerability, was shut down so the class could finish a definition.

The teacher, one of our school's racial equity leaders, was pulling some straight-up White-guy bullshit, the same kind of White-guy bullshit I pull all the time without realizing it. By insisting on a linear structure determined by me for an exceedingly complex and personal topic reflected in our students, the other White guy and I find it way too easy to say the word *race* a lot so long as we keep teaching in super super White ways.

But, hey, we're super antiracist. We can name the names, we can be angry at the failings of the school system, the justice system, and oh, don't even get us started on the media. In fact, do get us started on it so we can stand in front of a bunch of kids and tell them all the things we think about the way they are portrayed in movies and TV, and your comment is great, but let's stay on topic, because maybe we aren't ready to get that real yet, because maybe we aren't an expert in you and we want to stay the expert.

We feel that our anger at oppression entitles us to an opinion, but our entitlement is that oppression.

When the voices of people of color are being minimized and marginalized, when their experiences are being questioned, when their lives are being devalued, it is by White people. When conversations about race are being derailed or dismissed, it is by White people. When someone is saying, "I know your children aren't being fairly educated, I know they're being unfairly arrested, I know nearly every image they see of themselves is a negative one, but this isn't about race," it is a White person talking. It is White people, and it is arrogant, selfish, and ignorant for me to pause those conversations for one minute to say, "But not me."

We police Black voices with calls of being impolite, for being "unproductive" to White listening, for not bringing us along, for showing a fraction of the anger for large offenses that many White voices show for very small ones. We accuse them of being racist for conversations that name race, that don't make room for the devaluing of their children and coddle grown-ass White people who haven't found a moment in life yet to really think about race. We let White people not listen by attempting to translate messages that need no translation.

I will keep saying "we" because I am a White male. The purpose of identifying myself as such is to recognize that as a member of both identities I am tied to the behaviors, beliefs, and privileges of other people who share those identities, whether I like it or not. I need to understand what it is to be not only White but male, because not understanding does not make a single problem of privilege go away.

I am a White male. I rely on White privilege, often but not always, without recognizing it. I have been dangerous, often but not always, without intending it. I seek conversations that help me to understand my privilege, and I bristle at actually losing even small pieces of that privilege. When I am not given the chance to speak, I react poorly because I am used to every space being my space.

And even in schools where most of our students are people of color, our schools are often White spaces. And even in schools where most of our staff are women, our schools often have male staff, union, and administrative leaders.

I've seen disruption, pretty massive disruption, caused by enforcing dress codes on female students. Students often, and understandably, react poorly to being told that clothes they have on or body parts they have make them inappropriate for school that day. There are meltdowns, to be sure, and indignation. There is yelling and arguing and many things that are massive disruptions to learning. Sometimes kids go home for the whole day, which is a whole lot of learning not happening.

I've seen administrators enter active classrooms, walk around the room sticking their heads under desks to look at the length of skirts and shorts. Really, in the real world, I've seen this. I've seen girls asked to stand up in front of classes, looked up and down, and then told, "Yeah, I guess you're okay. Sit back down." I've watched administrators leave, and then I cared for embarrassed, shamed, angry students. I've seen whole days of learning disrupted, and that doesn't take into account the emotional damage done to students by a system that should be protecting them.

I'm uncomfortable with the message we are sending. Kids are self-conscious enough. Girls especially have enough people commenting on how they look and holding them to an often impossible and moving target of appropriateness, attractiveness, and self-expression. I don't like a school telling someone that the clothes they put on their own bodies made them a problem for the whole school they attend, so much so that they need to go home or cover up. So much so that they need to feel shame. Shame disrupts learning more than skirts. I promise.

We're more comfortable confronting the girl wearing the thing, and not the boys who say the things about her. We are comfortable putting the blame for the actions of boys onto the girls around them. We support a culture of shame in our schools. We support a culture that says that female bodies are not their own, that females are responsible for the actions of others with regards to their bodies.

I don't do that. I swear that I don't. I don't think that I do, and until I was confronted by my student about how big of an ass I can be sometimes to female voices in my room, I would have been sure I was pretty much nailing it. There were men out there that were sexist and shitty, but not me. Not all men, right? So long as I wasn't the one enforcing a shaming dress code, surely I was one of the good guys, right?

WAY BACK at that conference group of White guys, I thought hard about what words truly describe White men in the world. I called out, "Dangerous." Dangerous.

The group didn't like that, because no one in the group would describe themselves individually as dangerous, but by "Not all men"-ing our understanding of what it means to be a man in the world, we imagine that we are somehow immune to the effects of harassment. We can imagine that unless we are active rapists and harassers, that our presence in the world isn't somehow shaped by rape culture, and that our microaggressions of gaze, of bad jokes, of objectification don't somehow feed and support that culture.

We need to recognize the experience of girls and women being objectified, catcalled, attacked. We need to recognize our role as the predator, the role as the rapist. We are the person most likely to rape and kill the women around us.

I may say a simple "Hello" to a stranger, and she may feel harassed. But can a simple hello actually be called harassment? Yes. For two big reasons: one, because she said so, and shut up and listen when people say they feel harassed or offended; and two, because I am not the first man to ever say hello to that woman, and so my interaction carries the weight of other interactions with other men. I should know, if I am listening at all to nearly every one of the women around me, that they have had interactions that started with a hello and have ended in someone invading their space, in someone saying something disgusting, in someone meeting silence or polite refusals with insults, with threats of rape, with "Bitch."

Those interactions carry weight into our classrooms. Those interactions are reinforced by teachers who give equal room to guys who say that women shouldn't be offended by them.

It doesn't matter how many times I've seen *The Notebook* or what feminist writers I follow on Twitter. My intentions don't matter; my history doesn't matter. In that space, I am dangerous because I'm a man, because men are dangerous in those situations. I should know this. There's no excuse not to know this.

White men. We are the beneficiaries of a dangerous, reckless amount of privilege. We are the violent defenders of any threat to that privilege. We are the default, the assumed norm, the humanity through which others are denied full humanity.

As a White teacher, especially as a White male teacher, I am the instrument through which many students are introduced to their own marginalization. Any time I spend not recognizing that, any time I spend hoping that if I ignore it, it will just get better, any time I spend not supporting, protecting, and amplifying marginalized voices in my room is just straight-up White-guy bullshit.

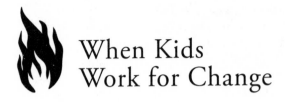

When Kids
Work for Change

I HATE DRESS CODES. I don't see how we have any business as a place people are required to be to tell them how to look when they get there. I don't like schools used as an instrument of shame or cultural supremacy.

I hate dress codes, but not nearly as much as a group of girls in my school hate them. The group, which started after one of those "we're going to go to class and talk about how shoulders are the devil and will make all the boys murder each other and also not do their homework" talks that come around whenever it gets above sixty degrees in Minnesota. As the dress code was applied—unevenly, unfairly, and unkindly, as usual—the group turned from middle fingers under the desk to a full-fledged school movement with a logo.

They called themselves the Feminist Killjoys, and it is impossible for me to love anything more than that.

Through protest and persistence, they did what so many resistance movements in school fail to do: they created change. They pushed their peers and many staff members to see things differently, and they impacted school policy. Both the what and the why of the dress code shifted. It kicked ass.

Students have come to me with all sorts of issues, and it is a powerful and important thing that teachers do to coach their students through bits of life outside of their room. Sometimes, those bits of life include the chance to learn how to stand against what you think is wrong, stand for what you think is right. Sometimes, kids just have to fuck shit up because they're the only ones smart enough to realize how shitty the shit is.

When students come to me complaining about the things in school that drive them nuts, the garbage that stands between them and the school they deserve, I do my best to give them the tools to change what they can without telling them why or what they should change. Basically, and radically, I talk to them like they are real actual people who can make decisions and stuff. Also, I have a lot of faith in young people right now, and they have a lot of work to do to make things better in the world they're building for themselves, and school is a great place to practice.

Creating change in a system that celebrates the status quo is a challenge, and giving the right advice to students (without taking over for them) can make all the difference. What follows is a somewhat formalized version of the advice I give to the kids who care enough to be pissed.

DISCLAIMER

Actions have consequences. Challenging existing power structures is not an activity often met with ice cream parties and awards. You may have people frowning at you. I cannot promise there are not punishments that go along with some of the things I will present as options. It's on you to do things right, to know your school and its rules, and to act in ways that you are ready to accept responsibility for. Hopefully, doing the first options of change well will remove the potential "You're in trouble, Mister" options from the table.

This information is intended for (and, really, only useful for) positive action to create a better school. Schools are not perfect places, and sometimes can be wholly awful places. Though our families trust our schools to give their children what is best for them, they sometimes need to be pretty loud about just what that is. Though it should not be the students' responsibility to fix things, sometimes nothing will happen until the wisdom, energy, and organization of young people make it happen.

KNOW YOUR POWER

When I was in high school, I was a pain in the ass, and I was loud about it. Some things I did well and were helpful, and some things were annoying enough to distract and deter from the intended goal. Now that I've been teaching for a decently long while, I wish I could send a letter to that kid with the pink hair writing articles and organizing protests in his friend's basement. That's what this kind of is.

Let me tell you a secret that I doubt is really a secret. Schools are scared of kids. Kids make schools difficult places to run, difficult places to work in. Kids are so human, so full of feelings and histories and constantly evolving lenses through which they see their world. Teaching would be easy if there weren't people involved, but there they are, leaving their backpacks in weird places, and falling in and out of love and hate, and getting in actual tickle fights with the person next to them, and then looking at you like, "Well, why aren't you teaching?"

Frustrating though they may sometimes be, students are by far the most powerful group in any school. The whole scale of humans in the building and their power is actually the reverse of what you'd likely think. Administrators sure seem like they've got a lot of power, but their power, like a lot of power, is really dependent on what people are willing to let them do with it. A student alone can only do so much, but in a thousand ways a day, students show that together they can make a school do whatever the hell they want it to do. Teachers are somewhere in the middle, often far too subject to school happening to them, also gifted with direct connections with kids all day long. Those moments, those kid-to-teacher moments, are the envy of so many administrators and district personnel and lawmakers who wish they ultimately had a fraction of the immediate impact on students that teachers have every day.

I think teaching is pretty hard. In fact, the book you're holding could really be titled *Welcome to the Shit Show, Plus Jokes.* Teaching is tiring and frustrating work, but it's work. It's a place I go to and a place I leave. I think about teaching a lot when I'm not at school, but I don't really need to.

Yes, teaching high school is pretty hard, but going to high school is a whole heck of a lot harder. Going to high school means being surrounded by high schoolers, plus teachers, plus administrators and parents, all with a thousand expectations on how to act, dress, feel, think, not to mention what to read, what to write, and when, and how. When you leave the school building, most of those expectations are still there. Except for summer and select exceptional weekends, school is an unfairly large chunk of your whole life. So it's worth having a school that you like. Sometimes, that means screwing with the school that you have.

Also, students should understand that they have the right to a school that does not suck. School sucks sometimes because it's school, or because you're a teenager, or because life. Sorry. That said, you do have rights.

You have the right to a positive environment.

You have the right to be free from embarrassment, shaming, or screaming in your school day.

You have the right to have your identity, your passions, and your personal history affirmed.

You have the right to be heard.

You have the right to good classes, good teachers, and work that is good for you.

You have the right to be weird and still be treated like you belong.

You have the right to use changing your school as practice for changing the world.

IF YOU FEEL like any of those things aren't happening, then you have the right to ask and then demand and then work for and then jump up and down and stomp your feet until those things happen.

Here's how.

UNDERSTAND YOUR SCHOOL

Before you start making change in your school, you need to understand as much as possible about how your school works. This means understanding how the system works, what you can expect as far as support and resistance from people in different roles, and, above all else, just how much power students have. So let's start there.

It's easy to imagine that students are at the bottom of the power ladder in a building. They are subject to more rules with less input than anyone else, which is why there is so much work that needs to be done. Students have things like detention and suspension; they are subject to grading; and as individuals they need more from their school than their school needs from them.

Remember: a single student may struggle, but a group of students is the most powerful entity in a building. Really. I promise. It's true, and schools hate when students start to figure that out. Schools are given exactly the amount of power students collectively allow.

Like I said, I was a pain in the ass when I was in high school. I started an underground school newspaper that was critical of school policies (plus jokes). I organized protests against deteriorating art budgets and fought the school on the censorship of materials in the library. (Remember that *Rolling Stone* cover with the *SNL* cast dressed as cheerleaders grabbing each other's bits? Yeah, they decried that cover as pornography and tried to have the magazine removed forever. After some lawsuit threats and school board protests, the [still ridiculous] compromise was reached of putting the magazine behind the counter, available with parent permission.)

In a district of around two thousand kids, about half the members of my school board knew me by first and last name, and I don't think it was because they liked me very much. Still, I didn't push nearly as much as I could have because I was scared of what they would do to me. Looking back from inside that structure, I realize now I could have done one whole heck of a lot more. When it comes down to it, there's almost nothing your school can do to you unless you break something or attack someone. Don't do those things.

Really, seriously, don't break stuff or hurt people. I'm not discounting the whole history of violent rebellion in the world, but as much as your school may suck, your school is not a tool of fanatical fascism. Your school is not stealing your family or cutting off any of your limbs. So long as you don't break the big rules, your school can do almost nothing but frown at you. You can't be suspended for disagreeing. You can't be suspended for asking questions or raising issues. Schools should treat students fairly and respectfully. If they don't, we can fight (but not physically fight) until they do.

Sometimes, that fight is easier if there are adults on the side of the kids.

It's unfortunate and ageist and ridiculous, but sometimes one parent in a principal's office is worth ten students. It's important to have parents because they may have easier access and a different audience. If the issue is the right sort of issue, you may find a friend in your school's PTO (Parent–Teacher Organization), and certainly they should be interested in the student perspective of whatever story needs to be told.

Teachers are pretty restricted in terms of open rebellion. This is my cop-out paragraph, and it's going to be full of the same sorts of cop-outs you will likely hear from lots of teachers. Many teachers have family and mortgages. It may be harsh, but they are not willing to risk those things to fight their bosses on hat rules. When I was in high school, I had a few teachers who I knew were friendly to my various goals, and those teachers were profoundly helpful for talking through my plans, in coaching my language on letters, and at least pointing me toward maps of the system I was trying to navigate. When I asked them about their bosses, they would often smile, say they loved their bosses and every decision their bosses made, and show me a picture of their house with their family standing in front.

In my high school, our fight was often with admin. Your situation may well be different, though, and those bosses, the administration, may end up being a great help to you. In fact, if you're planning on being or supporting a student activist, it is not a bad idea to seek a positive relationship with your administrators along the way. I've worked with some really brilliant people who run schools, and those people love to hear student voices and student concerns. Principals are people too. Reach out to them. Be respectful and calm and informed. Trips to the principal's office are a heck of a lot better when you've asked to be there in the first place.

Once you've understood the school you're in and the people around you, it's time to pull a chair up backwards with a cup of hot chocolate and have a nice healthy chat with your very own special self and whatever minions you've gathered to your cause. If you are angry, upset, offended, or passionate about your cause, your instinct will be to sit and complain about said thing. It feels good to say something is wrong in front of a group of people, and it feels even better when people in the room nod their heads. Don't get too caught up in this. You have work to do, and your first job is to ask the best possible questions.

ASK THE RIGHT QUESTIONS

What is the root of the issue?

Lots more questions. Is someone not being heard? Not being represented? Does the problem stem from mistreatment or from opportunities being limited? To really fix something, you have to know more than what it is: you have to know where it's coming from.

What do you want?

Don't stop at what you think is dumb, or what you think is wrong. Come up with a plan for how things could be better. Imagine the meetings you may have. Will you be focused on solutions? Will you bring new ideas to the table? I see this a lot in advocating for change in school discipline. I don't like suspensions and I want suspensions gone. Lots of people want suspensions gone and can speak at length and loudly about how suspensions should be gone. Awesome. But then what? What next? How do we create a system that isn't punitive and exclusionary and encourages positive growth and support for students? I've been in a whole lot of meetings where no one has an answer to that question, or where people just say "restorative justice" a whole bunch of times without any real plans on how to make that happen on a systemic level. Those meetings don't tend to go anywhere, but everyone really feels like they're getting some work done, so that's good, right?

People shut down quickly when all you are doing is telling them they're wrong, even if they are wrong. People get defensive when you tell them they've screwed up, even (and especially) if they screwed up. If you don't need to establish past problems, don't. Focus on moving forward. If all you're looking for is an apology, you likely won't get it, and if you do, an apology to you won't help the next kid.

Will what you're doing get you what you want?

Anger feels righteous, and breaking rules is pretty fun, but will it accomplish your goals? When I was a teenage rabble-rouser, I always wanted to jump first to whatever action was the most dramatic. Sometimes those things worked, but oftentimes it took a lot longer and a lot more compromise to change things after a loud, messy first attempt. Keep your goal in mind, and make sure your plan is pointed at achieving that goal.

The difference sometimes between things that work and things that don't is that things that work take people who work. A lot. It's actually pretty easy for a small group of loud people to disrupt the work of others, and the shouting and table pounding will ultimately feel like you're getting something done. It's way harder and less immediately rewarding to build something positive and cool, but the advantage is that you may well be adding something that makes your school better.

What is the scope of the issue?

Is this a classroom problem, a building or district problem? Is this regional, national, or global? If this is something just happening in your school, or just happening to you, you should look around and see if there are larger issues at play and larger groups you can ally with. If this is a global issue, finding global support may be easier, but you also need to figure out how you can make your issue personal and local to the people you are trying to convince. There is no problem too big or too small for good work to be done, but you should be aware of the size of the problem at hand.

Does everyone have all the information?

If students are taking issue at the actions of a single teacher, great. Before you move forward with massive protest, does that teacher know? Does their boss? Do they know, and do they know the whole story, and do you? You have strength in your truth, but you compromise that strength when you only share it in pieces, or when you tailor it to different audiences. Collect and distribute information to all stakeholders. Doing so may just make everything move that much better as you move forward. Information may solve the problem all on its own.

TAKE ACTION

Low-level ruckusing

Get Organized

You can do this, whatever this is, alone, I promise you, because you're a beautiful magical snowflake and everything is possible and you can totally change a whole system all by yourself. Still, you should figure out if you have any support, and you should bring those supporters together. Start a Facebook group, an e-mail chain, a Twitter hashtag—whatever works for the people you are bringing together. In drastic situations, you may also consider talking with real humans to their real faces. Organize your allies, your ideas, and your plan of action before you start.

Your group needs to decide:

1. What is the problem?

2. What needs to be done?
3. How should we do it?

Don't do anything until everyone involved knows the answers to those questions and how you came to them. Communication is organization, and organization is power.

Schedule a Meeting

There are few great, productive options when you start agitating for change. This means, like all great revolutionaries in history, you have to ask for a meeting. First and foremost, you need to give whoever has the ability to fix the problem a chance to fix the problem. Figure out who that person is, and then make sure that person knows who you are. That person may be a teacher, a staff member, a building administrator, a superintendent, the school board, or someone in the state government. When I was your age, you little whippersnapper, that meant writing a letter to a person who talked to the person who might be the person you want to talk to. Now, you have e-mail, and e-mail kicks the ass of all but the most ridiculous bureaucracies. E-mail someone in charge, introduce yourself, say a bit about the thing you are interested in changing, and ask for a meeting. If they don't respond in a day or two, e-mail again. If they don't respond again, or respond in the negative, find out who that person's boss is, and e-mail that person instead. Wash, rinse, repeat as necessary.

When you get a meeting, be sure to use it well. The person you will be meeting with will most likely be a professional-meeting-being-atter. They will want to drive the meeting to fit their needs. Walk in knowing exactly what you want to say and not say. Come with a plan, and look for resolutions. Don't waste their time, and don't expect that everything will get fixed instantly. They may need some time to think things over and talk to other people, and if you represent a group of people, you should make no final decisions without consulting them. There may need to be follow-up meetings, which may sound super awesome, but be careful. It's very easy to confuse having a meeting with actually doing something. Keep your eye on your goal, and keep working until it's done.

Meeting To-Do's:

1. *Know what you want said.*
2. *Be confident in your message. Be courteous in your delivery.*
3. *Listen to what they say.*
4. *If they promise to do something, write it down and remind them later.*
5. *Keep pushing.*

Go Public

If meetings aren't working or the people involved refuse to have them, it may be time to take your message public. The advantage of trying to settle things quietly and civilly before you go public is that all those unanswered e-mails are now ammo to prove you've done things right and have been ignored. If you aren't getting heard in private, go public.

Going public can mean lots of things. It may be that news media is already sniffing around the school and all you need to do is raise your hand and step forward; or it may mean you need to contact them. The problem with jumping toward the media first is that you are ultimately not in control of what they say. Someone's genie wish gave us the Internet (bless their heart), and you should use it. Write blog posts, start a Twitter or Facebook campaign. Be funny, be satirical, use art, use your brilliance. If you're not a professional communications person, don't try to sound like one. Sound like you, because authentic communication is way more powerful than hyperprofessional communication (that, and it seems like the job of most communications people, is to say as little as possible in as many words as possible). Make sure that anyone who can hear you knows you're someone who should be listened to. Sure, sometimes those people may also be media members, but unless your issue is "I'm never on the news," getting interviewed is not achieving a goal. You need to make sure it helps you get there.

Talking to the media is dumb because the media is pretty dumb, and also full of its own agendas and biases. In order to help them be helpful, you should make sure you (and anyone in your group who may get a microphone shoved in their face) have some talking points. What are the crucial things you want to say? Make it simple and say them over and over and over. Video and print media need to pick little clips of what you say, and your hour-long interview will be condensed down to fifteen words you only kind of said unless you give them those fifteen words over and over again.

But what if your fifteen words are great, but no one will listen? Well . . .

The Nuclear Options

Walk Out

There're a lot of reasons that Walkouts are dumb. Really. I'm not just saying that because I'm an adult and adults always tell kids not to be loud and ridiculous. They don't work because kids walk out and have no idea why. That kid, that one with the hair thing and the shirt and stuff, that kid? That's the kid the news is going to talk to, and there's no way that kid is going to say anything about your issue. That kid just hates Biology. I'm not saying don't do a Walkout. I'm saying if you're going to do one, you better work your butt off and take the time to do it well, or it may just make things worse.

Sit In/Occupy

Like a Walkout, if you're going to go here, you need to have all your ducks in a row, and then you need to be ready for your ducks to get into some serious trouble. If you've gotten this far and nothing has worked and the only way to fight the system is to disrupt it, fine, but do everything you can to think of a better way first. If you've done the work and there is some seriously unjust stuff happening and nothing is going to be okay until it is fixed, then, yes, sit right in the damn middle of that stuff and refuse to move until it gets better. Let me know. I'll come sit next to you.

MAKE CHANGE

Disruptive protest is a beautiful thing when it is done for beautiful reasons. If there is great injustice, fight it with greatness, with fierce courage. If the best brains around you are working with you, you can think of a better way to protest than ripping off the '60s. I've heard of schools where students hold workshops for teachers on issues of race and get the leverage from the district to force attendance. Go big, go loud, go brilliant and creative and wonderful. Celebrate the beauty of human voice and experience in the faces of those who would restrain it. Don't just advocate for change—that's what adults who are scared of losing their jobs do. Make change. Make it and refuse to accept the promise of it at a more convenient time.

Push and push until the wall gives way.

Part IV

SPRING

Like most things in life that prove this is all one
big bad joke, you will learn how to best reach
and teach your students right as they are getting
ready to leave. Do the hard work at school.
Don't avoid the places where you struggle;
lean into the impossible things about teaching.

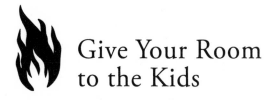 # Give Your Room
to the Kids

WHEN I TAUGHT EIGHTH GRADE, I often organized the graduation celebration. For whatever reason, even though it was just middle school, there was an hour-long arts performance, speeches, diplomas. There was a choir, a band, an orchestra. There was a reception with cake, with powdered lemonade in giant orange coolers, with three million pictures and seven million side hugs. There was honest-to-god sobbing.

In exchange for organizing, I was often allowed the privilege of avoiding some end-of-the-year stuff I'd rather not do, like watch musicals. I love art, I love kids. I love kids making art, and most especially love the idea of theater and performance and everything it does for the soul and the world. That said, I have never once been in a theater watching a musical and not wanted it to end. So, near the end of one year, middle school students were putting on a musical that was some modern retelling of some story I didn't care about anyway, and there was music and a clumsy house band, and I had many things to get ready for the upcoming graduation, so I got to sit in the hallway.

As I was shepherding kids into the theater, I grabbed a couple of backpacks away from students, backpacks being the harbingers of hot Cheetos and cell phones and all other things that get in the way of art. The kids went in, sat down to watch the what-have-you, and I sat on the floor with a laptop and started some comparison sheet-cake shopping. While choosing between cakes that looked like nonfood and other cakes we couldn't afford, I noticed a distinct smell coming from the bag next to me. The smell, most familiar to me from my days going to Phish shows (I don't want to talk about it), and from the moments just before my friend got kicked out of our freshman dorm (he'd rather I not talk about it), was unmistakably illegal.

I grabbed the bag and went to the office. "I'm about to find some weed," I told our assistant principal, "and I'd rather not find it alone." Weed was found, and the student was retrieved from the play. Bringing the bag to the office removed me from responsibility, which was nice, but also removed me from control of what happened next. While sitting in the office, the student was grilled (with real, actual anger and scariness) by an administrator who seemed intent on cracking a drug ring that did not exist. She kept signaling me to join in on the berating, and I tried to speak up in defense of the kid. Way too late.

The cops were called and they did some more scary yelling. The kid was sent home by way of the police station, and by the end of the day we were told the student would not be allowed back in our building. Ever. We were three weeks from the end of school and this student would simply be considered finished with middle school and sent on his way. He would not be welcome in the building for graduation, for the final dance, or as a participant or audience member for any of the final arts performances.

My team and I threw some fits but were ignored. We tried and tried to at least let the kid, the kid who had been a member of our school for five years, at least come to the graduation. Nope. As a final and fruitless show of protest, we read his name at graduation after being told not to and took a half-second to recognize the member of our community who wasn't there to join us.

I don't know. It was bullshit. It was bullshit, and I felt like it was my fault.

Looking back, I'm still not sure what I should have done differently. For a moment, I thought it would have been relatively amusing to take the weed from his backpack and flush it, but not say a word. He would know I knew, and I would know he knew that I knew, but we could leave it at that. I'm pretty sure I could get fired for that, though, and also pretty sure I should be fired for that, so it's a less-than-perfect option. I thought about different administrators I could have taken the bag to who may have handled it differently, or ways I could have at least tried to keep the cops out of it. I think a lot still about how I could have just ignored it, could have just smelled something from a bag that was mostly likely weed, decided not to make a big deal about it, and go back to a universe where shopping for crappy cake was the biggest issue of the day.

I'm not sure what's right. I'm not sure what I would do now if given the chance to go back. My best guess is that I would just let it go. Honestly, I don't think weed is that big a deal.

I STILL THINK ABOUT IT, years later, and continue to one-billionth-guess my decision. The backpack happened while I was in my fifth or so year of teaching, and I had fallen into an uneasy balance of being generally laid back about things while being an absolute hawk about broken rules and extremely talented at catching kids doing the stuff that kids do. In college, I worked at a record store (if you are unsure about what a record store is, use your Internets for fun, historical pictures of these crazy places). I was a goofball most of the day, would often skip half of the jobs I was supposed to do, was professional, friendly, and knowledgeable with customers, and was absolutely the best employee at catching shoplifters. Also, after catching them, I would often grab a few CDs and exchange them for a sub or some coffee with another college-age-degenerate-worker from a nearby business.

I was, on balance then, a pretty shitty employee.

I was, in my fifth year of teaching, pretty much the same way. I was a great enforcer of rules, a great breaker of rules, and a goofball in all the times between. After my zeal for enforcement led to a kid ending the day at a police station instead of school,

I started to really think about how power and enforcement are structured in schools, and remembered why I really hated being a student. It took me five years, which makes me kind of an ass-hole. I get that.

Recently, I was sitting with a coworker in a meeting of region-al minds calling for dignified behavior interventions in public schools (like ones that don't involve handcuffs). We were among the few teachers there, willing to work against our own power in the school system and work for schools that we would have wanted to attend. My coworker called the process (he was hit-ting it after only three years, the show-off) a "re-radicalization," which I liked. I called it "pulling my head out of my ass" but we meant the same thing.

It is so, so ridiculously easy to spend our time and energy as teachers making our job easier. Since our job very often feels impossibly hard, the time feels well spent.

In my state, teacher's unions started because schools were death traps for everyone in them. Teachers formed together and demanded, essentially, that someone come in and pound down the nails sticking out of the seats and quit heating the buildings by throwing oily rags on a pile of naked coals in the middle of the floor. It was a difficult fight, and one that makes me proud to be a unionista (which I think is actually a word, though I would prefer unioneer, as it suggests the addition of a rocket pack).

Our union still does much the same work, pushing for schools that are better because, at least metaphorically, there are still plenty of nails sticking out all over the place. Sometimes, we do other work that mainly serves to make my life easier. We say over and over again that what is best for teachers is best for students. More and more, I would like to see our narrative change, ever so slightly, by switching the order of the roles and demanding what is best for students, because it will be good for teachers.

The yelly rhetoric response goes, "You can't put students first if you put teachers last!" Good bumper sticker. What I'm trying to do, though, is just knock teachers (specifically the one in my classroom) down to second. In my own classroom, it has meant actively giving away power and decision making to my students. It's meant making my job harder.

For example (and you may disagree with my example, and so may I, by the time you read this, because I'm still figuring things out), I've essentially eliminated due dates on assignments in my room. There is a certain timeframe that we will work on a certain project and then move on, but students are free to continue working on that project until they feel done. That way, if all goes well, students are given the best chance to be the most successful on everything they hand in.

It's kind of a nightmare.

On due dates, about one fourth of my students hand their work in. That number gets better after a week, but there are always four or five students per class who do not hand anything in until they are absolutely forced by the end of the quarter to do so. This means that I very rarely get to sit and "get grading done" during a chunk of time, which is my favorite way to grade. I grade constantly, little bits at a time, across multiple projects. Constantly.

I could argue that the approach tires me out, and keeps me from focusing properly, and is therefore bad for students (though the extra time and flexibility have been very good for the quality of student work and the number of student breakdowns). I could argue that what is best for me are due dates with strict deadlines because I get to organize my life better, and a happy teacher means happy students. I could argue that, but it would be bullshit. Lazy bullshit. There are two reasons I honestly want to change. One, it's a lot of work, and two, it just doesn't feel like "normal" school. Reason Two is also why I feel I'm on to something.

I have colleagues who hate the approach (and likely aren't too keen on me in general). They say that I am not preparing students for college due dates and late-work policies. They are right: I am not. I would like to, but I would also like them to get into college based on their skill level, and strict due dates and late-work penalties were making some students who could create and think at an A level get terrible grades in class. I was also getting a lot more work that was half-done, or rushed, or just generally pretty crappy. I still get some of that work, but not as much.

I think my system works for kids. I grade them on what they're able to do so their grade reflects their skill in my class, not their ability to organize themselves or follow due dates. Those things are important, but my class is English, not English and Study Skills. It's a nightmare of grading and scattered assignments, but it's better for the kids I have, so I'm trying it out and trying to make it better.

Kids need more than better grades, though. We may forget it too easily, but it's really damn hard to be a teenager.

When you look at the structure of schools, it's pretty obvious that we plan our schools thinking of the system, thinking of the time and effort that will be put into management, and thinking of many sets of people before we think of students. If we were truly planning a school for students, for what is best for the reckless shit storm of adolescence, how long would the break between classes be? When would school start? What sorts of projects would we do, and what tools would we have to do them? I understand it would be nearly impossible to provide a school that is perfect for every individual student, but what if we actually tried? Actually held every adult in every building to a code where every conversation (even the ones where no one else is around) is actually centered on students?

I just finished a year with one of the most talented students I've ever had. I had the student in eighth grade, before I was moved to the high school in time to have him again in tenth and eleventh grades. As a middle schooler, he was a funny kid. He wrote short stories in his free time that he almost never let anyone see, and he drew with the same sort of furrowed, anxious mania that I adopt while writing.

This year, though, was different. During the very first day of school, he came into my room before class started. He told me that during the hour he may need to answer a phone call. If you could see the look he gave me, the glassy panic of his eyes, you would have said yes too. The call came; he went to the hallway quietly. A few minutes later, he was back in my room. A staff member had seen him on the phone and asked to see it. He showed them the phone, proving that it was a family member calling, but the staff member calmly hung up the call, took the phone, and walked away. The family member was calling, just by the way, from court, where the student's parents were fighting to keep custody of him. The staff member didn't ask that, though.

What followed that day, and much of the whole year, was a school so intent on system that it ignored the person being batted around by it. Within a month, the student was effectively homeless, living with almost no possessions in another city, taking public transit an hour and a half every day to and from school. His life, his daily, normal life, would be an emergency for any of the adults he came into contact with at school, and they all knew it, and they all kept marking him tardy, docking for late work, shaming for work undone.

The kid just needed a thousand hugs a day, and a little bit of credit for being smart as shit and having a really bad year.

In my class, he got that as much as I could give it. He was writing essays in eighth grade that would have gotten him A's in eleventh grade, so I wasn't crazy about super-long essays. I made sure he picked up the new ideas we were working on but never gave him anything to take with him when he left. I would check his grades regularly and would sometimes let him use time in my class to make up stuff from other classes.

Every so often, I would take him out to lunch so he could talk about his plans. He used what time and resources he could to start putting together a professional portfolio. He started lining up some places to show his work. He got himself enrolled in college classes while in high school so he could start getting credits before he had to pay for them. He knew full well that when he turned eighteen he would be on his own, and he was getting himself ready for it. With no real home, no money, and little more than was in his backpack, he was getting ready for the life he should have. Very, very little of what he did all day at school was helping him on his way.

I wondered often if I would give this treatment to all my students, or if it was just that this kid was this kid. I hope to hell I would. I hope to hell I do.

This treatment, by the way, was not just me going easy on him. What I was doing, or attempting to do, was going as hard on him as he needed me to be. What I was doing was trying to really meet the kid where he was and give him what he most needed from my class. That's different for every kid, and a ton of work to figure out and manage, but it's not anything more than we should be doing. Our kids are phenomenally good at telling us what they need so long as we're good at listening. But what would happen if we really gave our students the room to do what they wanted?

I mean, there are few things scarier to me than losing control over absolutely anything. This is true about everything from hall passes and seating charts to choice books and projects. Even, maybe even especially, when a student is working on something especially cool, my instinct is to butt myself in and make it even more cooler. I fight that instinct and am often rewarded when I give my kids that space.

Empowered kids are messy as hell, though.

I know how to do things the other way. I know how to do worksheets and checklists in a way that really feels like learning but pretty much isn't. I know how to get a classroom that is quiet full of kids doing today's task filling in blanks from the word bank. It feels like a thing, and it pulls the line up a little from the worst-case scenario of kids not doing anything in your class. Your best-case scenario, though, is nothing much better than completion. Most worksheets beg your kids to copy from one another and extend a hearty invitation to not worry too much about thinking today.

When pushing for more autonomy and creativity from kids, you may even hear them complain. I've certainly gotten "Why can't we just do a worksheet?" more than a few times, and good god, think about what that student is really asking. Their life would be easier, contained in forty-minute chunks of task completion, and my life would involve stacks of sheets to be graded off a master. And then what? It can feel like success, but we can all do better.

One of the best days of teaching I've ever had was the day I completely lost control of a classroom. On the last day of the school year, my juniors were taking a final. This final would be a culmination of that semester's work and worth at least a letter grade up or down in their final grade, so, you know, no big deal. Great day to lose control.

My final was pretty cool, too. Students were reading two articles written that week that both talked about students in our state. One was quite positive, the great potential of youth and how much we disserve them by expecting too little from them. They ate it up. Sweet. The second was from a local paper about all the problems at a high school a few miles away. That article was not so sweet and referred to the "taming" of students and generally cast young Black kids as inherently violent and scary, while extolling the White teachers who worked with them as blameless victims. My students spent the hour identifying word choice and phrases that built each piece's perspective on students and blahblahblah quiet-time finaling.

Well, most of my students did. In one class, we had about five minutes of quiet time before Arrie'Anna, from one corner of the room, shouted out, "Oh, hell no!" Within the next five minutes, the whole class was grouped around one big table and were absolutely demolishing the second article. As a group of young, predominantly Black students, they had heard these lies told about them all too many times to not catch the weight behind each assumption made in the article.

"We need to do something."

Not learn something, not complete something, do something. Do. So they did. They informed me, quite respectfully but firmly, that they wouldn't be doing the final that day. Instead, they were going to spend the hour working together to draw attention to the racist garbage in front of them and push a narrative of young Black kids that reflected them much better. They talked like this because I'm fucking awesome at teaching. (Just kidding! They really are that smart.)

I think I could have pulled them back if I really wanted to. If I held the grade over their heads and shouted them back to their seats and all that stuff, they would have done the final, but holy shit, why? Instead, they put together and revised an action plan that put their voices into the real actual world. Part of it was to tweet through the hour and include the writer of the piece and try to bring her to recognize the issues in what she wrote. They started by drafting tweets like "You suck and should never write anything ever," and "This is racist bullshit," and a sort of best of both worlds, "You suck and so does this racist bullshit." Their leaders forced revisions, though. They recognized that starting with rudeness and swearing was only going to hurt their point in the eyes of many, so they tried to strategize about what to say.

"Wouldn't it be fucking dope," said Arrie'Anna, one of the smartest kids I've ever taught and also one of the very very worst at turning in homework and also the central leader of this finals rebellion, and also a prodigious swearer, "if we just tweeted her words right back at her, just to highlight how dehumanizing it is?"

Everyone got on board, and the Twitter storm started. I sat behind my desk, mostly sure I wouldn't be fired on the last day of school and so ridiculously proud of my kids (who, it should be noted, entirely fulfilled the purpose of the original final by showing their mastery of that semester's central themes and skills, but whatever). The kids ran the show; the show ran better because of it. The final became a day worth remembering, and a day that validated their ability to lead and to engage in the real world. It was a small piece of a dream that schools exist entirely for kids, a small step toward a classroom, at least, where that can be true.

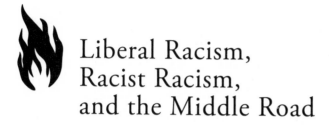

Liberal Racism,
Racist Racism,
and the Middle Road

I HAVEN'T BEEN A VERY GOOD TEACHER over the past few days. I've been quick to anger, the kind of anger that has led to my standing in front of the classroom speaking earnestly about why it's important to just, please, for the love of god, let me say one complete sentence.

Yesterday, a student was almost five minutes late to class. I let it go. The student started talking to the person next to her as soon as she sat down about a girl who said a thing to another girl who said something about that other girl who was a bitch. I asked for their attention for a moment. The student took out her phone, and I was done asking. I told her to put her phone away, look up at me, and pay attention. The student put the phone away and put her head promptly down on the table while not-so-quietly remarking, "Fuck this shit." I told the student to get her head up and launched into a speech to the class (but obviously directed at said student) about how the class is more than one person, about my expectations for behavior and engagement, how everyone needs to live up to at least the bare-minimum expectations of blahblahblah because we have real work to get done here, everyone.

I was being a pretty crummy teacher at that moment. I was calling this student out, and I could feel her anger growing to match my frustration. In the back, I saw a student nodding her head along with me. She was happy I was calling out a student who had disrupted many of her classes, a student who is more than occasionally open about not caring about school or anyone in it. The student in the back thought I was being a pretty great teacher at that moment.

So a tricky, weird, shitty part of me felt emboldened by the approval of the "good" student and justified in calling out the "bad" student. We were bonding in our Whiteness, and in our tacit approval of maintaining cultural Whiteness in the classroom. This shit happens all the time. It's hard to be honest about that part of me, it really is. It's really hard to be honest about how deeply racist dynamics permeate my teaching and classroom, but it's what happens, and most of my work revolves around trying to cut that shit out.

My journey as an antiracist teacher started in my very first years through open, challenging conversations with coworkers and students. When I was first introduced to equity work, it was through conversations with adults—intelligent, emotionally invested adults doing very good work. It didn't do a ton for me. Being raised in a nearly all-White town in what may well be the Whitest state in the nation (Wisconsin, the Polka State), I was defensive about race. When I started teaching (in Minnesota, the Other White State), I kind of just wanted the conversations to go away so I could go back to doing what I was doing. I learned the right things to say to get through it, but I wasn't really feeling it in my gut.

Later that year, my class combined with social studies in a "big room" of students engaged in very similar conversations about race and privilege. We gave them structure and a space and did very little as teachers over the next week other than point at who was going to talk next. I actually almost never did that. I listened and listened to my students explain how their skin color changed the way teachers saw them and treated them. I listened to young Black males recognize that they were rarely put near other Black males in seating charts and class assignments because they were seen as threatening when in groups.

I listened to students talk about being put in lower reading groups when the teacher found out their parents spoke Spanish. I listened to stories about suspensions, listened to stories of cultural supremacy masquerading as color blindness. I watched the faces of White students as their Black friends shared stories with the whole room that showed a reality they had never grasped. I watched as White students, catching on far more quickly than I did, were able to articulate places in their lives where they were given the benefit of the doubt, the automatic acceptance that their classmates weren't getting.

I began to understand Whiteness as a racial identity, that my skin color had often given me privilege and power, often without my asking. It's a difficult thing to understand intellectually during a conversation, but I found it even harder to carry my privilege daily in my awareness. I still struggle with that, with recognizing how race and culture can give a weight and history to a situation that I am not likely to feel.

I tried to apply my developing understanding to my practice and tried to structure my teaching in a way that worked against systemic racism. My first attempts were clumsy and counterproductive. I tried to connect the lyrics to "Drop It Like It's Hot" to the sonnets of Shakespeare. We studied the racism of World War II Germany and Apartheid South Africa without authentically linking it to student experience. It was effort without understanding.

I tried, oh how I tried, to be down with my Black kids. I sought the approval of my Black students as proof of my nonracist status. When Andrew or Brady walked by me in the morning, I would greet them, "Good morning," but when it was Julian or Latrell, I dropped my voice an octave and tipped my chin up and said, "What's up, man?" and I can't tell you how silly I sounded (and currently sound) when I try to talk, like, I'm a cool guy over here, I'm with it. While talking with colleagues who are people of color, I kept reaching for the right thing to say or do that would graduate me from equity work. That thing never came, so

I continued to grow (and grow, and push, and grow) and reflect on my practice, and I began to address race on a deeper level.

I added a quarter-long unit that studied and validated different dialects of English and focused on the concept of code switching between dialects. I use my class now as a way to teach students how racism operates, teaching them the concepts of marginalization, dehumanization, and misrepresentation. I try to give them tools to understand and dismantle racism in media, but I still struggle to infuse those lessons with concrete examples of how race operates in systems of power. I understand personal relationships as a key but see the difference between being a cool teacher and a respected one. I understand there is no set of mores, morals, or behaviors that captures every student from every cultural group, no certain reason that each Black, Brown, or White student acts the way they do.

Antiracist teaching is a process. It is a process without end, without a graduation and certification as officially antiracist, which is all the better reason to work with urgency. A fully antiracist school does not exist yet, and it won't until we figure out what one even looks like. Every step down the road is difficult. I'm constantly afraid of saying the wrong thing, constantly afraid of making mistakes, but I don't know another way. So I keep saying the wrong thing, keep doing some wrong things, and keep listening and reflecting when students are telling me something needs fixing.

White people (I being among the Whitest) are always reaching for how to lead things. We are the ones in the building who take the half-day equity training and then decide everyone else is mega-racist and we should be in charge of fixing them. We want to lead, because we are often handed positions of leadership, but, really, the most effective work I've done has been shutting the fuck up and making space for others.

I'M AT MY PARTICULAR POINT in my journey, and the view from where I am changes regularly. I have no idea if anything I think is right, but they're the rightest things I've found so far. This isn't a chapter of answers. I do not feel I've reached the end of the road, and I often need to turn around to pick up things I left behind. At this point, I am at an intersection in my practice, a sharp right or left turn, and I'm trying to figure out how to go down the middle.

The sharp right leads to a reinforcement of an already dominant White cultural norm. In terms of my classroom, it means that when a student is talking in my class, or openly defiant in any way, I respond with rigidity. One minute late to class means a call home. Talking while I'm talking? Step outside. Disrespectful when I talk to you outside? Down to the principal. The structure of school is designed to give me the power as the instructor to forcibly apply what some would call "classroom culture" or "school culture," but which almost always plays into quiet-is-best, compliance-is-respect, White cultural norms.

The sharp left is what is often called "liberal racism." This turn means that I recognize the many hurdles of microaggressions and the high wall of institutional, generational racism placed before my students of color. When they are a minute late, I say, "Well, strict time structures are not common in the cultures of people of color," or "My cool Black friend (I hope he's my friend) calls this BPT" (let me Google that quick to make sure that's what he calls it). When they are ten minutes late, I say, "Yeah, I guess that's okay, too." When they resist my calls for quiet, I say, "They are resisting White cultural oppression," and when they tell me to go fuck myself for asking them to put their phone away, I say, "Yeah, I guess I could have sounded kind of oppressive-y there."

I know that in the guise of "rigor" or "high expectations," it's easy to take the road right, and in the desire to be culturally conscious, the road left is full of instant rewards. However, the road right just makes the wall higher, and the road left doesn't build a ladder high enough to climb. The road down the middle is harder, because I'm not sure what it looks like.

The road down the middle means that my room is a safe space for kids that includes their cultural identity. It means I have relationships with students that allow me to push them to reach their potential while allowing room for their voice and some repairing of damage done from systems that have too often told them they are capable of less.

It's so damn hard, and it's hard to admit that it is hard, because so many of the clichés we throw around ("If you raise your expectations, your kids will meet them," "Give respect, get respect," "Focus on strengths") make it sound like it should be easy.

This girl, the girl I was calling out in front of the class yesterday, is a Black female with issues I cannot begin to comprehend. She's new to the school this year, and our awkward attempts at relating are overwhelmed in balance by our battles. She can be verbally abusive to other students, sometimes to the point of threatening. She's also smart, really smart, and failing almost every class. Some days she seems to care a lot. Some days not so much. Some days are really bad days, and there is something in her eyes that hits me right in my parent spot. The thing is, she makes it clear she doesn't want my help as often as I offer it, which doesn't make me stop offering.

Here's the other thing. This girl scares White teachers and knows it. Had I pushed one more little bit, she would have started yelling loudly and inappropriately (she could swear competitively, if that was a thing). The end result of the outburst would have many times led to her being sent to the office (I don't believe in it unless violence is involved) or the teacher backing off and doing exactly nothing. No things. Both options reinforce the behavior, and so, consciously or not, she had learned that loud anger, even when she's not particularly angry, is a handy tool to do what all of us really wish we could do, which is whatever we want.

I've seen what I really think is false anger from her on a few occasions. Of course, nothing is actually that cut and dry, because I've seen very real anger from her as well, and it's impossible to reduce the anger to the inciting incident. Some days, a snide remark from a teacher or another student is the tenth snide comment too many that day, the final shifted weight that releases an avalanche of anger built in the walls of school and beyond. Some days, the anger isn't nearly so deep. Ultimately, it's impossible and inappropriate for me to be the one who judges whether her reactions are authentic or not, but I do think it's important she develop coping mechanisms beyond anger for difficult situations.

I don't know what to do for this kid. I don't want to get into battles, because I'm scared to win them and I'm scared to lose them. When I don't confront her most destructive behavior, it only persists, it only expands. I think I could bend and twist and beg and shift and get her to do okay in my class—I've gotten good enough at that—but I don't think it would help her do much better in whatever class comes next, or whatever will come five years from now.

In the very middle of calling her out, just gaining momentum for what was sure to be a fantastic and predictable speech on how important it is to listen to every perfect word I ever say, and in the middle of recognizing the reinforcement of school as a place that isn't for her, I stopped. As is often the case when I am tired or frustrated, lessons that should have been learned before I ever had a class to myself finally kick in minutes after a confrontation actually starts. These are not the conversations to have in front of a class, and if you are asking for a student to listen to you who would rather throw something at you, asking them in front of thirty people is not how it's going to happen. I dropped it, got the class started, and after a few minutes, asked the student to talk to me in the hall. I had given her few reasons for her to do so, but she came. We talked over what happened. I asked her what I did to get her so upset. I really listened when she talked. I said my own piece about wanting her to do well. I tried to be specific about which behaviors (swearing and texting, mainly) I saw hurting her ability to do her best. I didn't want to reduce problems to *behavior* or *attitude,* because I've seen those words used too often to mean too many things.

I also talked with her about anger. I tried not to accuse, but I told her what my perception of her behavior sometimes is. She agreed that she sometimes acts angrier than she really is. I told her I would always let her address her anger, but that her anger would never scare me away. I told her that she was smart, really smart. I told her that she could get more from school than she was getting, and if she wanted to at any point, I would love to help her do that. In the mean time, I told her, I would love to see her involved in class as best as she could be, and if she was honest about when the bad days were really bad, I would trust her honesty and give extra room on those days. I wasn't being a great teacher yet, but I repaired most of the damage of being a bad one on that day.

Today was a pretty good day with her, but that doesn't mean more than that today was good. This has been and will be a journey of a thousand questions a day, hundreds of humans who have their own human things going on, and lots of mistakes. There will be so many mistakes, the occasional win, a few steps down the middle road.

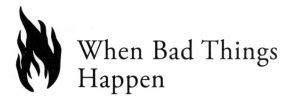

When Bad Things
Happen

THIS WEEK AT SCHOOL, someone threatened to kill me.

On Monday night I was sitting on my couch and watching some sporting game. It was late and well past my bedtime when I got a call from my principal. This is not a normal thing. He told me there had been a gun threat against the school, and my name was mentioned. I hung up, opened another beer, went back to the game. My team won, so all things considered, it was a pretty decent night.

On Tuesday, they gathered staff and told everyone about the threat. The teachers who knew I was the target gave me weird looks throughout the meeting. Teachers wanted to know about armed security and locked doors. When the meeting ended, I went down the block and bought myself a cookie, and it was pretty good, still a little warm.

On Friday, my principal came to me and said I had to decide if I wanted to press charges or not. I didn't. He said I should read the e-mail with the specific threat made against me. The e-mail was pretty specific about just what caliber bullet was being wished through my skull. The student said something about how it would be awesome if I got shot in the head. My principal asked me what I thought, and I told him I disagreed and thought it would not be awesome at all if I got shot in the head.

I left then, because it was lunchtime, and I had pizza. Also, I struggled to breathe right, thought it would be a good day to go home and lay down, but didn't.

No matter how much I liked to pretend it wasn't that big of a deal, how much I tried to invalidate the threat, the intention of the student, and the ability of the student to carry out that threat, I was sincerely fucked with.

On the same day the student made the original threat at school, that student said in a meeting that I was one of his favorite teachers, a "chill" guy. A week after the threat, that student, banned from the premises of the school, sent me a Facebook friend request. I have no idea what to make of any of that.

On a smaller scale, I've felt things like this before. Since we're all filled with so much sloppy human emotion, and since school has us often careening off walls and into each other like a pinball machine with a few hundred balls going at once, things go wrong. There are times that people hate you, or at least act very convincingly like they hate you. You may find out because things are posted online, or a complaint is made, or, most often, because a student is looking you dead in the face and tells you they hate you. It doesn't feel awesome.

There are a lot of reasons this can happen. It may well be that you've been a jerk to that student. It may be that, on reflection, you realize that you've been extra hard on them, extra rude, extra unhelpful, and it's time to figure out where you went wrong and apologize. Sometimes, that's all it takes.

Toxic relationships can be dangerous things and can be incredibly challenging to save and make healthy for your students moving forward. With a thousand or so students over a career, the chances that you will get by without a single student hating you are pretty unlikely. I've known teachers (all math teachers for some reason) who manage to pull it off by being remarkably warm, friendly, likable, and also just generally far better at teaching than I am. Jerks.

Toxic relationships are the most exhausting thing about teaching (tied with five other things). Kids who just won't let you win, kids who you won't let win. Kids who will say the exact worst thing they can think of at any moment, and you need to pretend you're not hurt, need to be there for them two minutes later when they need your help.

It is so hard to be a decent person in the moments when a student intentionally makes your life miserable. Think of the conversations you've had or heard when a teacher has said a kid "was testing me" or "was awful to me." It's so incredibly hard in those moments to realize that it is, almost never, about you. Rarely as a teacher will you have done much to deserve the toxic relationship you have, which will of course only frustrate you more, which will of course only help make things more toxic. The students don't see you stay at school late or turn down the party on weekends to grade or prepare. They do not see you at two in the morning, turning in bed, thinking about how, for the love of god, how are you going to get through to that kid? Because surely if they just gave Sylvia Plath a try they would be fine forever.

They don't see it, but you have to care anyway. We have no logical or moral alternative to giving a shit about a whole bunch of kids all the time, every year.

SO THERE WAS THIS ONE KID, and she wasn't even my student. She was in the year below what I taught, but I was asked to sub Band one day (which I am willing to admit I did not excel at) and this kid was in that class. I tried to strike up a conversation, but when I'm first meeting brand new kids, I come across a little too cheesy and earnest and "Hey, I'm a cool dude. See? Look at me doing cool dude stuff. I'm one of those cool dude teachers." She introduced herself, and I went ballistic because oh my god her first name is totally the first name of one of my favorite poets, and do you want to hear the whole story of that poet? Sure you do, because I'm a cool guy with interesting facts!

This happened years ago, but I did this same thing today, on the day I'm writing about it, to a student I was trying to get to know who got to hear a solid five minutes on how interesting it was that the assassination of Franz Ferdinand pretty much depended on a sandwich because . . . whatever . . . she didn't care either.

In Band, not only did the student not actively care about Stalin-era Russian poetry (I know, right?), she seemed to actively dislike me. She hinted at this by looking at me like I was a garbage pile and saying, "Yeah. I actively dislike you." I'm not a great sub.

There's this awful reflex I can have sometimes where I think, "Oh, you don't like me now? Let me show you how jerky I can really be." It took months, it took many months, to slowly stop being the cool guy teacher who is also the jerk teacher, and for me to stop seeing her solely as that girl who really really super did not like me. Eventually, we grew to get along and then eventually to have the sort of fantastic teacher-student relationship that seems so effortless in movies. She came to me when things were going poorly and when they were going well. My room was her safe space, and she was one of those kids for me who made hard days so very worth it. Plus, when we did the unit on Russian poetry, she almost cried during a lecture and then asked if she could borrow a book by my favorite Russian poet, who became her favorite Russian poet. That's not really a thing that happens in teaching, but it really happened this time.

That was two years ago, and just a week ago, she (in a different school from mine now) sent me an essay she wrote about me. While it did include the phrases "He thinks he's the best thing on two feet," it also included phrases like, "He may be an asshole, but he's the best asshole I've ever met."

I mean, if that doesn't bring tears to your eyes.

The bad stories in schools don't always end in happy stories, and the worst things that happen in school have nothing to do with Russian poets. Though they are often places of such great, great good, schools are sometimes places that are goddamn awful. Humans are not always especially fantastic to one another.

Students are not the only ones who are shitty at school. Most of the worst things that happen at schools, the actually criminal life-wrecking bad stuff, is done by teachers. But, you know, we try not to talk about that.

The subject is taboo among teachers, was never mentioned in my teaching program or in anything I've ever read about teachers. But you know, unless my state is different from your state, there are a few teachers every year who get caught having inappropriate relationships with students. I have no idea if anyone keeps track nationally of how many teachers have done this thing that everyone pretends does not happen, but those numbers would only represent those people who got caught, and those people who got close and decided to jump over the line. So this thing, this thing that we pretend doesn't happen that often, is actually happening way too often in way too many places to way too many kids, and no one I've heard talking is talking about how to make it stop.

During my first year teaching, I was contacted by two different teachers, both were also struggling through their first year. Both were having feelings toward a student and called me for help. One called because he knew I wasn't judgmental and needed someone to talk him down who wouldn't tell him to quit forever. The other called because she knew I wasn't judgmental and wanted someone to tell her it was okay to flirt with a student. She was disappointed in my response.

Let me review, just in case you think you may have read that last paragraph wrong: two different teachers called me during the same school year because each was thinking about pursuing a sexual or romantic relationship with a student. Also, and I want to be extra clear about this, there is no such thing as a "romantic" relationship between a teacher and student. There is no such thing as a consensual relationship between an adult and a minor.

The first teacher was a quiet, awkward kid with fluffy blond hair who dressed like he had been tucking his shirts in since he was three. He got into teaching because he liked books, because he had liked every teacher he had ever had, and he thought it would be a good fit to teach kids like him. He got a job at a suburban high school and dove headfirst and full-time into a land of bored entitlement that nearly crushed him out of the profession. He struggled to connect with his students and felt mainly like he was wasting his and their time. The exception was one girl, a junior, who thought he was just the best teacher ever.

This girl gave him permission to feel like he was being successful somewhere in his job. She asked him for book recommendations and read everything he gave her with enthusiasm. She started spending a lot of time in his room, and sometime in early winter he called me. He recognized some of their behavior as flirting and was worried about the messages he may be sending, as well as the feelings he was actually having.

Before we decry this guy as a filthy pervert who should be dragged behind a school bus, let us cheer his bravery here. To call someone else and ask for help is a hard thing to do. To call and ask because of something like this must have been incredibly difficult.

I told him a few things. I told him to recognize the fact that he was young, that he had been in high school only about five years ago, and that when he was there, he was likely not getting attention like this from girls like this. He agreed this was true. He said, "She's the exact kind of girl I wished I was dating when I was in high school." I asked if he had done anything, said anything directly, even, that had crossed a line. He had not, but he had thought about it.

I told him to recognize the difference between thinking of unthinkable things and doing unthinkable things. By thinking about them, he had not fucked up someone else's life, or his own, for that matter. By doing them, he very well could. I told him he had to stop walking the line, because the line is a dangerous place. No more conversations after class, no more friendly chats. He had to cut the relationship off to a strictly professional relationship between teacher and student.

He was worried doing so would hurt her feelings. He was worried doing so would negate one of the only areas of success he was having as a teacher. I told him both things would likely happen, but they were the right answer. She will find other people to support her. You will find other kids you connect to. This relationship is unhealthy, I said, and needs to be shut down.

Also, I told him, I promise you I told him and was very clear when I told him, that this girl was a girl, a child. She should be dating other children, and any relationship, even a nonphysical, flirty relationship between a child and an adult, can be hugely destructive to that child. I used the word *child* a lot. I also offered my belief that any teacher–student relationship, even those between adults, was unhealthy from the start because of the profound power differential in its start.

Run, I told him. Run away from the line. You've done nothing wrong by finding an attractive person attractive and supporting a person who needed help. I worried he would see himself as having already broken the barrier, and so going any step further would be not that much worse. I thought about devout Christian teens who are less likely to use contraception because they're already breaking the sex taboo.

You know what he did? He ran. He checked in a few months later. The girl had finished his class at the end of the semester, and he had gone weeks without talking to her. The end. He's still teaching and seems to be doing a pretty good job.

The other teacher was a slightly different story. This teacher taught at a boarding school in the middle of nowhere. Most of the other teachers there had been there since before the world was in color. There was one other young woman she connected with, but most of her social interactions were with the students she lived around in the dorms. In other words, it was just a complete shit show and an awful idea of a place.

Most of her story was pretty similar to the other teacher. She was struggling to connect, struggling to feel successful. She and a male student, a senior, connected while she worked on a play he was cast in. He was bright, funny, talented. She told me, "He's the exact kind of guy I wished I was dating when I was in high school." Yep, and now he was giving her the sort of attention she never got as a student, and didn't it just seem like not that big of a deal?

I gave her almost the same advice as the other teacher, teamed with the advice of "Get the hell out of the boarding school and live among the wordly world." She offered most of the same retorts to my advice. If she shut down the relationship with this kid, it would really hurt him, and he's the only student she feels really gets her right now. As long as they walk the line without crossing it, it will be okay.

Run, I told her. Run away from the line.

She said I was right. She said she would follow my advice. She called me halfway through the summer. She had done nothing with the student during the school year. When he stayed on at the school as a counselor in their summer program, he spent the summer flirting with her and the other young teacher and left at the end of the summer to move back home. The relationship between the two teachers was damaged because they fought over the affections of this (barely) former student.

Fucked. Up.

That school, by the way, is responsible for about half the cases in the news over the past few years here of teachers sleeping with students.

Do not teach at boarding schools. Do not go to boarding schools. Do not send your children to boarding schools.

The wider point, other than avoiding boarding schools (and I do, again, recommend that you avoid boarding schools), is that as the adult in the situation, it is your responsibility to manage your relationship with students. They are children, and you are there to coach them as best you can, protect them as best you can, and deliver them to whatever their next step is. They are not about you. They are not there to redeem any unresolved issues from your childhood. They may act like real grown people, and they may look in some ways like real grown people, but they are, all of them, little babies to be protected.

Because you are paying attention (right?) you already put together some of the key pieces that link the two stories (right??). Social isolation is a real thing for teachers, for nearly every teacher everywhere. That isolation can happen because you accept a job far away from your friends and family, or simply because for many many hours out of the day, you are talking to people who don't have a driver's license. That social isolation can make social interactions with students some of the only outlets you have during the day, and those interactions can become inappropriate if you aren't careful (*inappropriate* here meaning the stories above, but also just unprofessional conversations about your co-workers or bosses, or other students, or how you used to smoke weed, too, bro, so it's all good).

Seek social support at school. *Social support* means, you know, friends. Try to have those. You may find, especially in your first job, that you are closer in age to your students than to many of your coworkers. Make old people friends. Old people friends are pretty cool, too. Old people friends can also remind you to keep the age and situation of your students in perspective.

If you see something, say something. For real. If you are worried about a teacher in your school and their behavior, let people know. It's possible that other teachers may find out you were the rat and be angry at you, and it's possible you may be mistaken, but you know what? Teachers are less important than kids, and if you think a kid is in danger, don't do nothing. I was a first-year teacher when my colleagues reached out to me, and I was reasonably sure that neither was going to act on their worries. Still, if it happened again now, I would do a lot more.

Ignoring the worst things that happen in our schools will not make them go away. Many people who enter teaching with energy, enthusiasm, and talent leave teaching after a few years. There're a lot of reasons why people leave, but none of them is that teaching is way too easy.

I Quit

EVERY YEAR, somewhere around this time, I decide to quit teaching. I get exhausted with teaching, with the adults I work with, with the kids who always need everything to be a thing. I get exhausted by the gap between what we ask teachers to do and what we give them to do it with. I get tired in a way that makes me want to cry without reason.

Most years, the decision to quit teaching is hollow. There is not a long line of noneducation suitors interested in someone who can make Shakespeare interesting and who would like to spend their day just, you know, helping people and stuff.

This year, the threat is more real. My school is shifting districts (long story), and staying in my same room teaching my same kids means making less money than I would have (longer story), and less than other districts are offering. There's also this piece where I've been spending a lot of time this year writing for and talking with a bunch of adults, and there're a few different people interested in having me do that full time in some way.

So I've been waking up early just to have some time in my classroom with a cup of coffee to sit and think. I've been staying late just to sit at my desk and pretend I'm reading something. I've been standing back and staring in the distance. I've been holding my head in my hands in meetings a lot. I've not been sleeping well.

A week ago, I quit teaching.

I decided I would find myself a job where I could do the work I do outside work at work. I would write, study schools and culture, try to understand, support, and fight for the decolonization of classrooms and the progression of teachers. There's work there that I think is important, and work that I think I would be good at. Also, if someone offered me a cabin in the woods to sit and write stories and essays that were increasingly out of touch with reality, I would take that in a second.

I didn't tell anyone I quit, but my mind was made up.

This wasn't a new experience. The first time I decided to quit teaching was about halfway through my first year. At that time, I co-taught a unit with a social studies teacher in combined classes, which meant two adults and sixty kids. Not just sixty kids—sixty eighth graders. Sixty eighth graders in the oasis of pain that exists in the month and a half before spring break where there are no days off of school, no end to winter in sight, and few reasons to feel really successful.

One thing that happens when school gets hard is that more and more teachers seem to be sick, which means more sub jobs than subs, which means school gets even harder. One thing about having two teachers in one room, even a room with sixty kids, is that from the front office it can seem like you have an extra teacher who can be pulled. During one week, my co-teacher was pulled for three straight days to cover another classroom, and I was left, woefully outnumbered, to do my best.

The kids weren't even that bad. Really. The kids were kids, were middle schoolers with their own issues and who talked a little too much and didn't always stay completely on topic, and I could not handle it. I've learned a lot since then about choosing my battles, learned a lot about deciding which hills are worth dying on.

To use another weird war metaphor, teachers need good armor. We understand, generally, that kids are kids and aren't finished being all-the-way-real people just yet. We let things, even sometimes pretty shockingly rude things, bounce off of us, because that's what we do. We build that armor with patience and love and reinforce it with self-care when we can manage it (like yoga, you know, or whiskey). Our armor keeps the work from getting to us, keeps us focused on the moments we have with the kids we have.

The armor is awesome and essential, and, ultimately, tragically, permeable. It happens. Your armor peels away, something sneaks past and under, and all that patience sheds away, and every little thing is a big thing, and every big thing makes you lose your fucking mind. It happens. Kind of a lot sometimes, it happens.

My armor did not last three days with sixty kids. My armor did not last past lunch the first day. By the third day, I had quit. There was nothing, nothing in the world that was worth putting up with the awful things about teaching. The awful thing that pushed me over? A kid told me to chill out. Chill out? Did he see what I was going through? Kids who forgot their pencil AGAIN, kids talking during the movie, kids leaving, LEAVING WITHOUT ASKING, to go to the bathroom. Chill out? This is the goddamn apocalypse!

Without armor, it all felt so important. Without armor, I literally hit sixty miles an hour before I left the parking lot. My teammates questioned, legitimately, whether or not I'd be back the next day.

I made it home. I had ice cream, then whiskey, then ice cream (I'm going to go ahead and name that a Teacher Sandwich). I told my wife about all the awful things that happened that day, and she did her best to not make a face like, "That doesn't really seem like that big of a deal," which made me think about how maybe some of those things weren't a big deal.

The next day at school, a student found me in the hallway and handed me a wristband that said "Rad" on it. She found it at the bus stop and wanted me to have it. I put it on because I needed Wonder Woman bracelets. As I walked into class, a student saw it and asked where I got it. "Jess found it at the bus stop."

"A bus stop? Dude, gross. It probably has hooker spit all over it."

I don't appreciate people being disparaging toward sex workers, but something about the specificity of the phrase and the surprise of hearing the phrase "hooker spit" that early in the morning just made me completely lose my shit in the best way.

Kids are amazing and awful and hilarious, and I know that, and I forget that, and they remind me that, and then I'm back in.

SO I DIDN'T QUIT. Not that time. Not the time I had to break up three fights in one day. Not the time a parent called to tell me she wasn't sure her kid had learned anything in my class. Not the time that one guy I worked with sent me the three-page e-mail about all the things he thought I was doing wrong. Not any of the next twenty times that same guy sent essentially that same e-mail. Not the time I switched to a new school and that same guy contacted a coworker to tell her to make my life hell that year. Nope. Kept wanting to quit, didn't quit.

But then there was last week, the week I really actually quit.

But then there was this week.

On Wednesday, I was reading an article with my class ("From Lynching Photos to Michael Brown's Body: Commodifying Black Death"), and at the end of the day one of my students took over our room. For twenty minutes, this student spoke truth about being a Black male, about the fear and assumptions he feels increasingly as he gets older, about his passions to succeed, to "live greatness," and how often he is made to feel like shit, and how often he is told he isn't shit. He spoke with anger, with pride, with intelligence and hope, and with a broad perspective and understanding of our world, which was, after a decade of teaching, among the most impressive things I've ever heard.

After the hour, I sat in silence with my student-teacher and after he left sat in more silence by myself. One of the most powerful experiences open to teachers is to be really taught. No book, no training, no group has pushed me to grow more than my students have; nothing has come close to the sense of awe, the inspiration, the energy they give me. Students are incredible, and I want to be with them. I want to be there when they do amazing things.

Teaching offers that, and try though I might sometimes, I can't think of anything more important to do. I was offered a job once writing curriculum for training modules used by large businesses. I mean, that sounds fucking awesome, right? Doesn't every little kid sit around and dream of the day they could write copy that teaches people to push the right buttons and ask the right questions while operating a car wash?

The job isn't a bad job, and people who don't teach aren't bad people (in fact, many of them get to carry around the extra patience they save not teaching and get to be much better people than teachers), but I just don't get it. I don't get going to a job to make money, and I realize that sounds ridiculous. The training module job would have cleanly doubled my salary, just by the way, which is an insane thing to turn down.

In the past few years, quite a few of my former colleagues have moved away from my school. Reaching a level of understandable exhaustion with the system around us, they moved on to the calmer pastures of the suburbs (and students who live in developments with names like Calmer Pastures). The pull is real. The pull of a job where I get to just teach, where I could be that teacher for the kid just like me who needed that teacher while growing up in a place just like that. Let me be real in a way that is super fucking uncomfortable for me: I sometimes think about how much easier it would be to teach at a super White school. The language my colleagues have used is different. They talk about a move to more "stable" schools, schools with "a better reputation" or where teachers "focus on teaching." They mean White. I'm pretty sure they know that, and I'm pretty sure I get why they don't say it.

My job now is at the front lines of everything fucked about our country. My students are parts of some of the most at-risk populations in America, are living in systems that work to keep them poor and oppressed. I don't jump to use words like *oppression*, but, shit, on so many days the word doesn't seem strong enough.

My students' lives, especially outside of school, are not mine, and being around them every day does not give the right to tell stories about them. Plus, all the awfulness in the world that my students see doesn't make my house less nice, less warm, my kitchen less full of food. The truth is that I have gained so much from my students, and often because they are different from me. They make me and my life better, and so let me be clear that they do not make me tired, but watching their school sometimes suck sure as hell works to kick me out the door. The school doesn't work well, but only because the school isn't for these kids. It's a hard place to be, it's a hard thing to witness and participate in. In a million frustrating moments a day, I am being begged to quit.

But my students are beautiful, even when they're being god-awful. My school is a place of such power and inspiration, and also the reason I think too much and sleep too little. A job that isn't a roller coaster sounds nice, but incomplete.

Two years ago I was talking with a biology teacher who told me that teachers who can teach at challenging schools have no business teaching anywhere else, because those schools need the best teachers they can get. I only think about her saying that about three times a day. I think about her and the students I have been privileged to teach and learn from.

I'm staying. I'm starting over, ready to learn more and excited to teach again.

I'm not staying because my kids need me. I'm not staying to save anyone. Anyone who thinks they need to save Black kids doesn't know enough Black kids, or Native, or Latina/o, or immigrant kids. I'm staying for the honor of being there as they live greatness, for the honor of being with them, for the honor of supporting when they need it and getting out of the way when they don't. I'm not staying so I can mentor these poor new teachers. I'm staying so I can watch them change schools for the better, so I can see what great things the generation of teachers not raised on color blindness can do when they have classrooms, departments, schools all their own.

I'm so tired and so full of energy. I am frustrated and inspired. I'm a teacher, and that is why I teach.

Part V

SUMMER, AGAIN

Finishing the year feels impossible, and then it's over.
It is something you have done, and now there's this
thing you do, which is Teaching.

Everyone feels it at different times, but the work
becomes part of who you are. Your students shape
you, far past the point that they remember
what you taught them.

Let Me Tell You about These Kids

NOW IS THAT POINT IN THE BOOK where I should be thanking people. I have a ridiculously long list of people to thank, people who shaped how I teach, how I write, and how I write about how I teach. People who put up with me being an asshat just about all of the time.

I started bunches of times to do all the thanking. I listed a whole lot of people, and they were important, and then I started to run out of space, and I wrote something like, "And all the students along the way who were cool, you know, and stuff."

Not enough.

There couldn't be enough. I have taught more than one thousand kids in the past decade. One thousand people who touched my life and pushed my thinking and bought in, for whatever reason, to whatever ridiculous shit I was doing that day. One thousand students. That's insane.

The only thing I can think to do is to tell you about these kids. It's going to be messy, and I'm going to forget kids I shouldn't forget, which will be awful. It is an impossible thing, to tell you about these kids, but I have to try.

You know how when you say someone's name, like your partner or your parent or whatever, that name just means so many things? The name carries weight and history and emotion and complexity. That's what the names of these kids are like. Each one, and more than that. These kids.

Let me tell you about these kids—and know that nothing, not one word of any of this, would be done without these kids.

Let me tell you about Laura, Mary, Sarah, Mia, Sydney, and Max, this group my first year that kept me teaching even though I wasn't particularly good at it, who were supportive and fun and funny and did projects far beyond what I asked of them because they thought learning was fun and stuff.

And there was Aamina that year, who left me no doubt that I had students far smarter than I was, and Tess, who left no doubt that some were way funnier.

And there was Brady, who would tease me about being fat, but only because I teased him, and we would take turns pretending to cry and run out of the classroom. By midyear, he would spend entire lessons standing with me in front of the class, and we would do something kind of like stand-up and kind of like teaching, I guess. I suppose it should be said, I don't think I've said it yet, that I have laughed more, and more deeply, while teaching than while doing any other thing.

At the end of that year, at the end of the final, I asked for feedback from students about what they thought they might take away from the class, and what they thought I should change. This kid Darnell wrote me one of the most beautiful letters I've ever received, thanking me for the year and everything I did for him, for believing in him.

I mean, goddamn.

And that was just the first year, and just a handful of about a hundred kids from my first year. There are other years!

Let me tell you about Sophia and Monet and Betsy, who figured out in the first week they could pretty much do whatever they wanted in my class as long as it was funny or clever enough, and who almost never used that knowledge for evil.

And there were Robin and Mitchell, who continually made great things and were casually genius at just about everything. Plus Hannah and Makenzie, whom you should know, you should get to know them, because they are probably the best people in the world.

And oh my god, of course, let me tell you about Delaney and Miracle and Judaisha, whom we called the Philosopher, the Warrior, and the Priest (though I don't remember which was which), and who would not accept anything but my getting better at teaching, who pushed and pushed against the Whiteness of the school and my classroom and my teaching, who I would give the keys to the whole damn world to right now if I could.

And Alicia, who listens to bands so cool they don't even have names and are referred to by a series of shoulder shrugs and sighs, who somehow managed to deal with me three different years of school and still learn things about English, and who I believe in so hard it hurts, and I feel truly and honestly lucky to even get the chance to be around her, even though she kind of acted all the time like she thought I was a dweeb.

Which reminds me of the girls. I mean, these girls. Lamonda and LeLe and Amica and Elon and Kendall, who fought and fought us, but only for the right to learn everything they possibly could, only for the right to have access to every bit of success they deserve, only for the right to go to a school that values their brains and talent and their unparalleled ability to disrupt things that aren't on their level.

And shit! Oh yeah, she should be at the top with, like, fifty other kids, but Arrie'Anna, man. That girl keeps me angry at schools and hopeful about youth at all times. She's taken over my class and spoken with me about youth antiracist leadership, and if the world is ready for her, then it is just just barely, because this kid is on the way.

And of course La'Zeya and Dezi and Ana and Saturn and Julian and Derek and Naji and Koreah and Antonio and Anthonique and Jamal and Ndeye and Mira, and Evan and Forest, obsessed with early '90s rap who grew from fans to creators, and Latrell, my god, Latrell, who took over my class for a whole inspiring day and straight-up preached truth. That kid and all of the so many kids I met as high schoolers who made me love teaching high school.

And Emily and Emily and Emily and Emily and a handful of really great Elizabeths and dozens of (seriously, all individually awesome) kick-ass Emmas.

There were Priscilla and Maria, who wrote research papers in eighth grade better than anything I wrote in college (maybe not the highest bar) about shady governments in the countries of their heritage, then wrote second drafts that included all the swear words they wish they could have used in the first version to describe the corruption that they studied.

And Oscar, who took advantage of my rule that I would read any book and assaulted me with so many goddamn books about submarines.

And of course, Asyana and Liz, who never stopped inspiring me with the empathy behind their activism and the absolutely fierce intelligence they won't let the world not listen to. Oh, and they're funny. Like, crazy funny, the kinds of kids I would just go sit near on those days when I just needed to be around good people. Sometimes Asyana would come up to me in the hallway with her newest in a line of paintings and say, "Look how huge THIS uterus is!" So there's that. Both of those kids especially pushed me to think about how gender and sexuality are treated and represented in my class. They made me better, and I mainly just got to be there to be, like, "Great job," every time they did a new amazing thing.

And . . . this is hard. This is the hardest thing. There are so many kids. I hope you understand that. The kids give so much, they try so hard. When you teach with and not at them, when you listen and when you care and they get to be people and you get to be a person, then it is overwhelming. It is too much.

There are these artists you meet, these kids who make things that are impossible and who make all the things you made as a teenager seem ridiculous. Madeleine and Andrew and Amara and Tina and Corinne and Jeremy, whose art is beyond their years, whose talent is beyond imagination. Plus there's Maddy, who drew a picture in eighth grade that I loved, and who gave it to me at the end of the year as a gift after she denied me twenty times offering to buy it from her, and that picture is now a tattoo on my arm that reminds me of the power of teen artists.

In fact, Jeremy and his whole crew. Jeremy and Jack made just about the best thing ever handed in to me, a graphic novel about the wall between Israel and Palestine, and all their friends, Max and Jason and Max and Isaac, and I guess, even Graham, who created their own little world of nerdy weirdos, and we'd all go out for lunch together downtown when they were seniors and talk about video games and illustration and how dumb school was, and they all looked out for each other fiercely while teasing each other mercilessly.

And there's this one Emma, whom I met as a fourth grader, a nearly silent (and guillotine-obsessed) fourth grader, who was in my Advisory group. I saw her once a month from fourth grade through seventh and then taught her in eighth grade as a still mostly silent reader of every written thing and a delightfully snarky kid. I taught her again in tenth grade and again in eleventh and last year watched her graduate as an accomplished playwright, actor, and director.

And there's Sharee, who couldn't be less like me and couldn't be more like me, and who often is who I wish I could be because she's far stronger and smarter than I am.

And plus Amari and Alexis and Dana.

And then Cooper, Diego, Josh, and Frankie and Noah and Harrison, makers of the infamous "priceless" video. A group of guys who started out cool as hell and somehow only continue to grow into remarkably talented, wonderful, ridiculous humans.

And a kid named Eve I called Dwight and a kid named Sarah I called Al, and Tatron and Madbot and Applesauce and Wheeler and Franny, who I called Franimal, who was the first student I connected with as a writer, and who sometimes would touch base after a few years and say she was still writing, and thanking me for that, and kind of I could just retire right there and be happy, plus Omar who somehow draws a link between literary analysis in eighth grade English and the job he just got working on actual real spaceships and stuff. And let me tell you about

MikkyT, a bright shining ball of effort and hope and goodness in the world, the kind of kid who swung by once every few days in the years I didn't teach her just to say hey, just to get made fun of, just for a little encouragement on her way to great things.

But also Amara, who wrote a note saying that I helped her to question everything but herself and also has the most purely and powerfully artistic soul I've ever encountered, and Macailah, nationally known as a writer before she finished high school, because kids can do that these days and totally deserve it.

And there's Thomas, whom I have known forever and who was too much like me for his own good, and his brother Peter and his family, who knew me as a teacher of their children for nine years and were always full of support and jokes and questions. Oh, Thomas, the questions. Always with the questions and the politics and the figuring out of the world all of the time.

There are so many kids like that. Calvin who was working with nonprofits on real actual solutions to things, and Noah who joined a school board as its student member and who could be my boss right now and that would be fine, and Seth who found Social Justice in middle school and now works on campaigns that fight for it in the for-real world.

And Grace and Helena, who attack the whole world with a ferocious empathy that demolishes ignorance, and Charlie who attacks it with a wit so dry and biting that it stings and who consistently served as the only one in the room who got what I thought were my best jokes and who swore a lot but got away with it because everything they said was so damn smart and needed.

Oh, and families. Hey Zach, and hey Ryley. Hey Bre and Brittany, and hey Sarah and Katie and Mary and Greta, and hey Jordan and Zach, Mia and Kaya, Harrison and Julian, Alex and Hannah, Madeleine and Elsie, Miyabi and Skye, Jessica and LaTasha, Jenny and Kelly, and of course Luka and Kosmo, and all, every one, of the Smileys. You all rule, your families all rule. These kids.

I'm making mistakes now, scrolling around Facebook and old e-mails, realizing there will be not nearly enough space, and not nearly enough time, and it's overwhelming, it's amazing. It's teaching.

The result of a decade of devoting myself to kids is too many people I love and respect doing too many great things in the world and having done so many things to make my life and work better.

This book and my work cannot happen without these kids. These and hundreds more kids. There can never be enough thank yous. I could never tell you enough about them, these kids, for whom the whole damn shit show is so incredibly worth it.

Tom Rademacher is an English teacher in Minneapolis, Minnesota. His writing has appeared in *EdPost, MinnPost,* and on his blog, *Mr. Rad's Neighborhood,* and he speaks about teaching at universities, conferences, and TEDx events. In 2014, he was named Minnesota Teacher of the Year.

Dave Eggers is a novelist and screenwriter. He is the author of *A Heartbreaking Work of Staggering Genius* and the founder of McSweeney's, an independent publishing house in San Francisco, California.